Flavors of
Northern Italy

Violeta Autumn

Illustrations by the Author

101 Productions
San Francisco

Published by 101 Productions
834 Mission Street
San Francisco, California 94103

Distributed to the book trade in the United States
by Charles Scribner's Sons, New York.

Library of Congress Catalog Number 80-83215
ISBN 0-89286-164-9

Contents

INTRODUCTION 5

VINI 9
Wines

ANTIPASTI E INSALATE 14
Appetizers and Salads

ZUPPE E BRODI 30
Soups and Broths

PASTE E SALSE 39
Noodles and Sauces

RISO E POLENTA 63
Rice and Cornmeal

UOVA 71
Eggs

PESCI 77
Fish

CARNI 93
Meats

POLLAME 114
Poultry

VERDURE 125
Vegetables

DOLCI E PASTICCERIE 135
Desserts and Pastries

INDEX 164

ACKNOWLEDGMENTS

I wish to give thanks to the following individuals:

My husband Sanford and our son Kellar, whose enthusiasm and constant assistance in writing the book were invaluable and utterly necessary.

Dr. Giovanni Zuccarello, Italian trade commissioner in San Francisco, for selecting the right wines for each recipe and for his excellent advice and assistance in the wine sections.

Gloria Bussa, for her thorough and patient assistance in testing the recipes, and for sharing with me her *piemontese* family's recipes.

Paul Boynton Meserve and Dale Hawkins, who came to dinner to taste my recipes and tell stories of their life in Italy and who also provided knowledgeable help in historical material.

Dr. Giovanni Righi Parenti, poet, oenologist, historian from Siena, for his historical anecdotes and humorous stories.

Italian trade commissioners Dr. Maria Luisa Pisano in San Francisco, Dr. Giovanna M. Casinelli in Florence and Dr. Giuseppe Meschini in Venice, whose assistance opened many kitchens and guided me to sources of fine local recipes.

Above all, to the Italian people *mille grazie,* a thousand thanks, for welcoming me so good naturedly into the kitchens of their homes and restaurants, and for giving me so generously their favorite recipes.

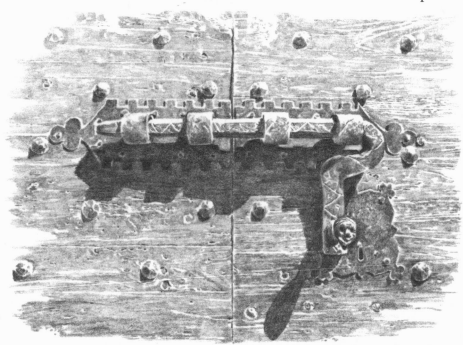

Ironwork on the gates to the Bargello, one of Florence's finest museums

Introduction

This book is an ambitious endeavor, for it attempts to realize Northern Italy as a living whole. To experience the cooking with its surroundings, I present drawings to depict the beauty of which the flavors are an integral part. With anecdotes, I hope to portray the warmth, humor and character of the people of which the tastes and treasures are expressions.

No one can go through Italy without being awed by the prolific production of masterpieces. The sheer number of art and architectural treasures everywhere is staggering. That Italians love their heritage is evident in all corners of the country. They are constantly and assiduously working at the maintenance and preservation of the works of art. Rarely do they miss the opportunity to travel throughout the country to visit the local treasures. Natives way outnumber the tourists in museums and historic buildings.

Most of the recipes and the sketches were gathered on an ecstatic three-month visit to Italy during the spring of 1978 with my husband and son. When I first visited Italy, in 1953, I was advised by my friend Eric Mendelsohn, "Don't photograph, sketch instead. Only that which you do with your own hand will you possess." There is much truth in the advice, for a drawing captures an emotional quality beyond the photographic. And if you go to Italy, take the book along—you may enjoy spotting the actual pieces of art.

You will find that this book is not a compendium, nor an encyclopedia of Italian cookery, but a collection of what I believe are the most enjoyable recipes of the region. They are *ricetti di popolo*, recipes of the people, as well as from *trattorie*, inns and restaurants frequented by Italians themselves.

Northern Italian cooking is subtle, it is varied and it is beautiful. Most recipes are deceivingly simple, compared with the richness of the results, and the pots are easy to clean. Northern Italian cooking differs from the Southern in a way that reflects the changing landscape, climate and cultural heritage of the two regions. As you move north the use of spices gets milder, tomatoes are added in smaller quantities and the cooking style becomes akin to Italy's northern neighbors, the French and the Austrians. In a further tendency to lighter cooking, contemporary Northern Italians are utilizing sesame and corn oils instead of exclusively olive oil.

ORGANIZING AN ITALIAN MEAL

Any dish in this book can be served within the context of American meals, but if you want to serve a total Italian meal in style, you may want to follow the general directions that I suggest and the guidelines on wines on page 9.

First and foremost you must get into the right frame of mind and allow plenty of time. Italians don't rush a meal, they savor it, take their time and talk a lot.

The table must be covered with an immaculate and well-ironed tablecloth. Don't be too elaborate with your centerpiece at lunch, flowers will do. For dinner you can have candles or another elegant focal point. Cloth napkins, silver, plates, glasses, bread and wine should all be laid out before the guests are ushered to the table.

Present the courses at the table one at a time (unless you are serving a meal *in piedi,* on foot, or buffet style where everything is in view). Don't rush to get the next dish; a slight pause to build up suspense and expectancy for what is to come is well received and well worth it.

Food is generally served in trays or bowls and passed around the table for each guest to serve himself. But I have attended dinners where the hostess served the food on the plates, which were passed from guest to guest around the table. After each course all used plates are removed from the table and a set of fresh plates is laid out for the next course.

ARRANGING A MENU FOR LUNCH

Start things off with decoratively served cold antipasti of the uncomplicated variety, like slices of salamis, prosciutto, anchovies and pickled vegetables. If you are serving cocktails before lunch, you may serve the antipasti at that time.

Next comes a dish of rice or pasta served *asciutto,* or dry, not in broth. Or you may serve an egg dish or a hot type of antipasto instead. In any case, the serving should be small, since the main dish is yet to come.

The main course comes in the form of a meat or fish served by itself or with a *contorno,* a side dish of vegetables.

Complete the meal with dessert, fruit and a *demitasse,* or tiny cup of strong black coffee.

ARRANGING A MENU FOR DINNER

As with lunch, start off with decorative antipasti, cold or hot, or both. Follow with a soup or *pasta in brodo,* not too generous an amount. Next you may serve a fish dish.

Then follows the main course of meat with or without a *contorno,* a side dish of vegetables.

Complete the meal with fine cheese and fruit, dessert and a *demitasse* of strong black coffee.

Small statue on lower frieze at San Marco in Venice

I Vini
Wines

To make an Italian meal truly successful, a wine should be selected for each dish so that they complement one another. And when serving the different wines certain guidelines should be followed to insure their maximum enjoyment.

Besides the suggested wines given after each recipe and the information before each section, I offer here some practical suggestions of a general nature on selection, storage and serving of wines. I should emphasize, however, that the choice of wines depends also on the preference and experience of each individual, as well as the particular circumstances and atmosphere one wishes to create. The task of choosing wines to accompany the meal is an art. It cannot be taught, but it can be directed along general lines, leaving the final details to the inspiration of the individual.

First of all, it would be an error to acquire a wine a few hours before the meal, or even a day or two in advance. Wines, especially quality wines, should be allowed to rest in a cellar at least ten days before being served. If you don't have a cellar, any other place will do, as long as it is rather cool and dark, and far from vibrations. I would discourage using a garage for wine storage: Unpleasant and persistent odors may be transmitted to the bottles. Except in the rarest cases, bottles should always be kept lying in a horizontal position, taking care to place them upright a few hours before opening. This will allow any sediment to settle at the bottom.

Dry white wines should be served cold, from 50° to 54°F (10° to 12°C), rosé wines at about 57°F (14°C), young reds at about 64°F (18°C) and older reds at around 68°F (20°C). Sweet dessert wines should be served at a temperature ranging from 57° to 64°F (14° to 18°C), depending on the type. For white wines, lengthy storage in the refrigerator should be avoided to prevent breakdown of the wine due to precipitation of tartrates. Refrigeration therefore should be limited to between one half hour and forty-five minutes, the time necessary to bring the wine to proper serving temperature. The ideal, of course, would be to place the bottle a half hour before serving time in an ice bucket that has been filled with ice and cold water. Wine should never be served with ice cubes since the melting ice would dilute the wine, totally altering the aroma as well as the flavor. Since white wines (unlike reds) do not need time to breathe, they may be opened immediately before serving.

It is said that red wines should be served at room temperature. Oftentimes, however, homes are either too warm for serving young red wines, which require a temperature of 64°F (18°C), or too cold for serving older red wines, which require a temperature of 68°F (20°C). It is best, therefore, to find a room in the house which has the closest desirable temperature, better a few degrees higher than a few degrees lower. Young red wines should be uncorked a half hour, or less, before serving. For older vintages and those with more body, a much longer period of time is advised, even up to three or four hours before serving. Here also, it is difficult to give a precise rule since so many variables must be taken into consideration: the type of wine, the area of production, the vintage and the producer. Once again, it is personal experience that must often be the deciding factor.

When opening a bottle it is best to use a classic opener, in order to avoid perforating the cork completely and to prevent cork residuals from falling into the wine. About a half glass should be poured out of the bottle to increase the surface area of the wine (in the bottle) that will come into contact with air. In case one wishes to speed up this process, or if one fears the wine has produced sediment, it is best to decant the wine in a carafe with a wide mouth, taking care to pour the wine slowly against a light source. This way, any sediment can be perceived and prevented from passing into the carafe. If one prefers, after a half hour or so, and after having washed and dried the original bottle, the wine may be poured back into it. Otherwise, it is suggested that the original bottle be brought to the table, along with the carafe, to give those at the table an opportunity to view the label and read its information.

Each wine should be served in the appropriate glass, and care should be taken never to fill the glass more than half way. This permits one to observe the wine against the light, to swirl the wine and to enjoy wholly its bouquet. Preferably, glasses should be crystal and never tinted. Tulip-shaped glasses with a high stem and narrow mouth are best for serving white wines, while red wines require glasses with a wider mouth. For dry spumantes, sparkling wines, fluted glasses that are tall and narrow should be used, and for sweeter types, including Asti Spumante, the preference would be a chalice-shaped glass, although not everybody is in agreement with this opinion.

Regarding the selection of wines to accompany certain foods, the general rules should be kept in mind. White wines precede reds, and younger reds precede older vintages; wines with a lower alcohol content and less body should be served before those with a higher alcohol content and fuller body. Also, the standard rule of serving white wines with fish dishes and red wines with meats should be exercised with some degree of flexibility. For example, with particularly delicate and subtle preparations of veal or chicken, some white wines are the perfect accompaniment, while for certain fish dishes prepared in heavier sauces, lighter red wines, such as a Bardolino or Grignolino, would be appropriate

Above all, be at ease, be flexible, and enjoy your wine and food.

D.O.C. WINES BY REGION

Italian wines of superior quality are labeled *Denominazione di Origine Controllata* (D.O.C.). The following list of D.O.C. wines by region is published courtesy of the Italian Wine Promotion Center in New York.

PIEDMONT

Asti Spumate
Barbaresco
Barbera d'Alba
Barbera d'Asti
Barbera del Monferrato
Barolo
Boca
Brachetto d'Acqui
Caluso Passito
Caluso Passito Liquoroso
Carema
Colli Tortonesi (Barbera, Cortese)
Dolcetto d'Acqui
Dolcetto d'Alba
Dolcetto d' Asti
Dolcetto delle Langhe
   Monregalesi
Dolcetto di Diano d'Alba
Dolcetto di Dogliani
Dolcetto d'Ovada
Erbaluce di Caluso
Fara
Freisa d'Asti
Freisa di Chieri
Gattinara
Gavi or Cortese di Gavi
Ghemme
Grignolino d'Asti
Grignolini del Monferrato
   Casalese
Lessona
Malvasia di Casorzo d'Asti
Malvasia di Castelnuovo Don
   Bosco
Moscato d'Asti
Moscato Naturale d'Asti

Nebbiolo d'Alba
Rubino di Cantavenna
Sizzano

VALLE D'AOSTA

Donnaz
Enfer D'Arvier

LOMBARDY

Botticino
Cellatica
Colli Morenici Mantovani
   del Garda
Franciacorta Pinot
Franciacorta Rosso
Lugana
Oltrepo' Pavese (Barbacarlo,
   Barbera, Bonarda, Buttafuoco,
   Cortese, Moscato, Pinot red,
   rosé and white, Riesling,
   Sangue di Giuda)
Riviera del Garda (Rosso and
   Chiaretto)
Riviera del Garda Bresciano
Tocai di S. Martino della
   Battalglia
Valcalepio
Valtellina
Valtellina Superiore (Inferno,
   Grumello, Sassella, Valgella)

TRENTINO-ALTO ADIGE

Alto Adige (Cabernet, Lagrein,
   Malvasia, Merlot, Moscato
   Giallo, Moscato Rosa, Pinot

Bianco, Pinot Grigio, Pinot
   Nero, Riesling Italico, Riesling
   Renano, Sauvignon, Schiave,
   Sylvaner, Traminer Aromatico)
Caldaro or Lago di Caldaro
Casteller
Colli di Bolzano
Meranese or Meranese di Collina
Santa Maddalena
Terlano
Teroldego Rotaliano
Valdadige
Valle Isarco (Muller Turgau,
   Pinot Grigio, Silvaner, Trami-
   ner, Veltliner)
Vini del Trentino (Cabernet,
   Lagrein, Marzemino, Merlot,
   Moscato, Pinot, Pinot Nero,
   Riesling, Traminer Aromatico
   di Termeno, Vino Santo)

VENETO

Bardolino
Bianco di Custoza
Breganze (Bianco, Rosso, Caber-
   net, Pinot Bianco, Pinot Nero,
   Vespaiolo)
Cabernet di Pramaggiore
Colli Berici (Cabernet,
   Garganega, Merlot, Pinot
   Bianco, Sauvignon, Tocai
   Bianco, Tocai Rosso)
Colli Euganei (Bianco, Moscato,
   Rosso, Spumante)
Gambellara (Recioto, Vin Santo)
Merlot di Pramaggiore
Prosecco di Conegliano-
   Valdobbaidene

Soave
Recioto Soave
Tocai di Lison
Valpolicella
Recioto della Valpolicella
    Amarone
Vini del Piave (Cabernet, Merlot,
    Tocai, Verduzzo)

FRIULI-VENEZIA GIULIA

Aquileia
Collio Goriziano or Collio (Cab-
    ernet fr., Cabernet Sauvignon,
    Malvasia, Merlot, Pinot Bianco,
    Pinot Grigio, Pinot Nero,
    Riesling Italico, Tocai,
    Traminer)
Colli Orientali de Friuli (Caber-
    net fr., Cabernet Sauvignon,
    Merlot, Picolit, Pinot Bianco,
    Pinot Grigio, Pinot Nero,
    Ribolla, Riesling Renano,
    Refosco Nostrano, Tocai,
    Verduzzo)
Grave del Friuli (Cabernet fr.,
    Cabernet Sauvignon, Merlot,
    Pinot Bianco, Pinot Grigio,
    Refosco Nostrano or Pendun-
    colo Rosso, Tocai, Verduzzo)
Isonzo
Latisana

LIGURIA

Cinqueterre
Cinqueterre Sciacchetra'
Rossese di Dolceacqua or
    Dolceacqua

EMILIA-ROMAGNA

Albana di Romagna
Bianco di Scandiano
Colli Bolognese Monte San Pietro
Gutturnio dei Colli Piacentini
Lambrusco Grasparossa di
    Castelvetro
Lambrusco Reggiano
Lambrusco Salamino di S. Croce
Lambrusco di Sorbara
Monterosso Val d'Arda
Sangiovese di Romagna
Trebbianino Val Trebbia
Trebbiano di Romagna

TUSCANY

Bianco della Valdinievole
Bianco di Pitigliano
Bianco Vergine Val di Chiana
Brunello di Montalcino
Carmignano
Chianti
Elba Bianco and Rosso
Montecarlo Bianco
Montescudato
Parrina
Rosso delle Colline Lucchesi
Vernaccia di S. Gimignano
Vino Nobile di Montepulciano

MARCHES

Bianchello del Metauro
Bianco dei Colli Maceratesi
Falerio dei Colli Ascolani
Rosso Conero
Rosso Piceno

Sangiovese dei Colli Pesaresi
Verdicchio dei Castelli di Jesi
Verdicchio di Matelica
Vernaccia di Serrapetrona

UMBRIA

Colli dei Trasimeno
Orvieto
Torgiano

LATIUM

Aleatico di Gradoli
Bianco Capena
Cerveteri
Cesanese del Piglio or Piglio
Cesanese di Affile or Affile
Cesanese di Olevano Romano or
    Olevano Romano
Colli Albani
Colli Lanuvini
Cori
Est! Est! Est! di Montefiascone
Frascati
Marino
Merlot di Aprilia
Montecompatri Colonna
Sangiovese di Aprilia
Trebbiano di Aprilia
Velletri
Zagarolo

ABRUZZO AND MOLISE

Montepulciano d'Abruzzo
Trebbiano d'Abruzzo

CAMPANIA

Greco di Tufo
Ischia Bianco
Ischia Rosso
Ischia Bianco Superiore
Solopaca
Taurasi

APULIA

Aleatico di Puglia
Cacc'e Mmitte di Lucera
Castel del Monte
Copertino
Locorotondo
Martina or Martina Franca
Matino
Moscato di Trani
Ostuni
Primitivo di Manduria
Rosso di Cerignola
Salice Salentino
S. Severo

BASILICATA

Aglianico del Vulture

CALABRIA

Ciro'
Donnici
Pollino
Savuto

SICILY

Bianco Alcamo or Alcamo
Cerasuolo di Vittoria
Etna
Faro
Malvasia delle Lipari
Marsala
Moscato di Noto
Moscato di Pantelleria Naturale
Moscato Passito di Pantelleria
Moscato di Siracusa

SARDINIA

Campidano di Terralba or
    Terralba
Cannonau di Sardegna
Carignano del Sulcis
Giro' di Cagliari
Malvasia di Bosa
Malvasia di Cagliari
Monica di Cagliari
Monica de Sardegna
Moscato di Cagliari
Moscato di Sorso-Sennori
Nasco di Cagliari
Nuragus di Cagliari
Vermentino di Gallura
Vernaccia di Oristano

A young Bacchus assisted by a Pan in the courtyard garden of the Palazzo Reale on Via Balbi, Genova

Antipasti e Insalate
Appetizers and Salads

Eating, to Italians, is never a rushed affair but an experience to be savored slowly, fully, always happily and, if at all possible, in company. The antipasto is the way to start things off in a colorful and relaxed way. Antipasti can be hot, cold, or a combination of both. They can be intricate concoctions or simply a platter of cut raw fresh vegetables to be dipped in an oil and vinegar dressing.

Salads take a confusing role in the Italian menu. There doesn't seem to be any set place for them. However, a few general rules, sometimes contradictory, can be applied. Never have wine and a salad made with vinegar served together. For a meal with many courses, the salad may be served after the main course. A salad many times can be considered equivalent to the antipasto. I have included the salad with the antipasti because we Americans are more likely to eat the salad at the beginning of the meal.

WINES AND ANTIPASTI

Wines to be served with antipasti follow one basic rule: They should be dry, white wines with a low alcohol content. This rule applies whether the antipasto is based on fish, meat or sausage. The only exceptions are antipasti that are heavily marinated. In such cases, if drinks are served, it is best to restrict them to mineral water, which tends to eliminate the strong flavor of vinegar and prepare the palate for the wines that are to follow. In a few cases, a highly refined antipasto may be served with a dry spumante.

If you are giving a party where the fare is constituted entirely of many different and elaborate antipasti, it is preferable to offer a variety of wines, leaving the choice to your guests depending on which antipasti they select.

FAVE CRUDE
Raw Fava Beans

As a child I used to enjoy chewing toasted dry favas that almost broke your tooth. I have always been fond of cooked favas in soups, salads, and with butter and lemon, but in Florence I learned to eat them raw and love them. The chef at Trattoria Silvano was eating them himself for lunch one day, and kindly shared some with me. Favas are usually available in summer in well-stocked American supermarkets. *Salame toscano* has larger pieces of fat than other types of salami. Pecorino cheese is made with sheep's milk. Both the salami and the pecorino are sold in markets catering to Italian cooks. You may substitute any Italian salami and a sharp, salty cheese.

1 pound (500 g) fava beans in their pods, very fresh
1/2 pound (250 g) *salame toscano*
1/2 pound (250 g) *pecorino toscano* cheese

Wash pods and drain. Place in serving bowl. Slice salami very thinly and arrange in serving plate. Serve the pecorino almost whole, with just a few thin slices cut from it and a sharp knife beside it. Allow people to shell their own favas.

Serves 6
Serve with no wine

INSALATA DI FINOCCHIO E POMODORO
Fennel and Tomato Salad

1 head fennel
2 large tomatoes, cut into wedges
1/4 cup (75 ml) olive oil
2 tablespoons (30 ml) red wine vinegar
Dash garlic salt
Salt and freshly ground black pepper to taste

Remove hard outer leaves of fennel. Cut in quarters lengthwise and wash thoroughly. Dry with paper towels. Cut into thin slices. Arrange fennel and tomatoes on serving plate. Blend oil, vinegar, garlic salt, salt and pepper. Pour over vegetables.

Serves 4 to 6
Serve with no wine

INSALATA MISTA
Mixed Salad

1 head lettuce
1 cucumber
1/2 fennel head
1/2 carrot
1 garlic clove, halved
1/4 cup (50 ml) olive oil
1 1/2 tablespoons (25 ml) red wine vinegar
Salt and freshly ground black pepper to taste
2 tomatoes, cut into wedges

Wash lettuce leaves and pat dry thoroughly; cut into bite-sized pieces. Peel cucumber and thinly slice. Cut fennel into bite-sized pieces, wash and dry. Peel carrot and grate into long strips or shave into thin curls. Rub the inside of a bowl with garlic clove and place in it all vegetables. Blend oil, vinegar, salt and pepper and pour on vegetables at time of serving. Toss gently. Garnish salad with tomatoes. You can also serve salad without dressing and offer oil, vinegar, salt and pepper at the table.

Serves 4 to 6
Serve with no wine

*A street in Assisi. If you walk down
these steps and turn to your left,
you will find the house where Saint
Francis was born.*

CAVOLO MORBIDO
Wilted Cabbage Salad

1 firm green or red cabbage
1/4 cup (50 ml) olive oil
2 tablespoons (30 ml) red wine
 vinegar
Salt and freshly ground black
 pepper to taste

Remove tough outer leaves from cabbage. Wash, drain and slice very finely. Add other ingredients. With one hand work the cabbage a couple of minutes to soften it. It comes out tender and with a pickled quality.

Serves 4
Serve with no wine

INSALATA DI RISO DI FLORA GROSSI
Rice Salad

4 cups (1 L) water
1/2 teaspoon (3 ml) salt
2 cups (500 ml) long-grain white
 rice
7-ounce (200 g) can tuna fish
1 small can anchovy fillets in
 olive oil, drained
1 red bell pepper, cored
1 slightly green tomato, thinly
 sliced
1/2 cup (125 ml) olive oil
Salt and freshly ground black
 pepper to taste
1/2 teaspoon (3 ml) chopped
 fresh sweet basil
1 teaspoon (5 ml) chopped fresh
 parsley
2 hard-boiled eggs, sliced
6 or 8 green olives

In saucepan bring water with salt to boil. Add rice, stir once, reduce heat to low, cover tightly and allow to steam for 20 minutes without removing lid. Turn heat off. In 5 minutes rinse rice under cold running water. Drain thoroughly. In serving bowl place rice, tuna and anchovies. Add bell pepper and tomato. Dress with mixture of olive oil, salt, pepper, sweet basil and parsley. Toss to distribute dressing. Garnish with hard-boiled eggs and green olives.

Serves 6
Suggested wine: Orvieto, Soave, Alcamo Bianco, Lambrusco

PANZANELLA
Old Bread Salad

This recipe is meant for a summer day. However, it was a spring day in Siena when the matron of our hotel gave it to me, as one of her favorite salads. Our hotel fronted a minute piazza, one of the many nooks that make up this medieval town. The cobblestone streets are so narrow, the town patriarchs were compelled to be environmentalists and so banned the car.

On our first evening, after a full day and with full stomachs, we retired early, only to hear our piazza full of sound: the murmur of voices and the bustle of footsteps. How foolish to go to sleep and miss all the activity. We hurried to our window and looked out. There was no one in sight, but the sounds were still there. From then on, each early morning and late dusk, we would delight in listening at our window. Through the prevailing stillness and intermittent flutter of pigeons' wings, we would hear, but not see, a crowd of sound. Voices bounce on the bricks and stones and flow through the crooked streets like the wind. It is impossible to say where the voices come from and soon, you wonder whether they spoke in the present.

Palazzo and Piazza Salimbeni, Siena

1 head lettuce
8 slices 3-day-old french or italian
    bread
2 tomatoes, cut in wedges
1 cucumber, thinly sliced
1 large red onion, thinly sliced
4 leaves chopped fresh sweet
    basil, or 1/2 teaspoon (3 ml),
    crushed dry basil
1/4 cup (50 ml) olive oil
2 tablespoons (30 ml) red wine
    vinegar
Salt and freshly ground black
    pepper to taste

Wash and dry lettuce and cut into bite-sized pieces. Cut bread into bite-sized cubes, sprinkle them with cold water enough to dampen but not to soak. Add tomatoes, cucumber, onion and lettuce. Add oil and vinegar and season to taste.

Serves 6
Serve with no wine

CALAMARI COL SEDANO
Squid and Celery Salad

This recipe comes from the two chefs at Antica Carbonera in Venice. When Umberto gave me the recipe, Riccardo begged to differ in the type of oil. Riccardo maintains that olive oil is a bit too strong for this dish, and just about every other dish as well. He recommends cold-pressed sesame oil.

The only parts of the squid that are edible are the tentacles and the white sacklike body. The insides, skin, eyes and mouth part are discarded. If you are making *riso nero,* or black rice, then you should search inside for a silvery, elongated small sack containing the ink.

1 pound (500 g) squid
3 stalks young tender celery,
    thinly sliced
3 tablespoons (45 ml) olive oil
    or cold-pressed sesame oil
2 tablespoons (30 ml) white wine
    vinegar
Salt and freshly ground black
    pepper to taste

Clean squid (page 88) and boil for 30 minutes. Drain and slice into thin rings. Rinse in cold water, drain and refrigerate. When well chilled add celery, oil, vinegar, salt and pepper.

Serves 4
*Suggested wine: No wine. But if
    you substitute fresh lemon
    juice for the vinegar you may
    serve Soave, Pinot Grigio or
    San Severo Bianco.*

GRANSEOLA IN GUSCIO
Crab in its Shell

This handsome dish also comes from Umberto and Riccardo, proprietors of the *trattoria* Antica Carbonera, near the Rialto bridge in Venice. When I asked them to share this recipe with me, Riccardo did, in the grand manner. He brought in his hands a *granseola*, the beautiful long-legged crab of the Adriatic, and cracking it open proceeded to show how the dish is done. As a final touch he took a scoop of the brilliant red eggs of the crab and placed it on top, completing a dazzling visual effect. This crab is endemic to the Adriatic only, so a large ordinary crab will have to do.

On the southeast corner of the Ducal Palace in Venice, near the Ponte della Paglia, you can see this sculpture of the Drunken Noah. It is a Venetian Gothic high relief in Istrian limestone, done in the first half of the fifteenth century. Noah's children and the Bridge of Sighs are around the corner.

1 large cooked crab, well chilled
2 tablespoons (30 ml) olive oil
2 tablespoons (30 ml) fresh
    lemon juice
Salt and freshly ground black
    pepper to taste
1 parsley sprig, chopped

Clean crab (page 91). Take care
not to break the shell that covers
the body. Wash shell well and
keep in refrigerator. In a bowl
put the white meat from the
center part and legs. Chop but
do not mince. Add oil, lemon,
salt, pepper and chopped
parsley. Stuff mixture into the
clean shell. Serve in a tray of
crushed ice or simply cradled in
lettuce leaves and surrounded by
cherry tomatoes.

Serves 2 to 4
Suggested wine: Pomino, Greco
    di Tufo, Ischia Bianco

ACCIUGHE FRESCHE MARINATE
Marinated Fresh Anchovies

This tasty recipe comes from the
family of Laura Ponzanelli in
Florence. A variation of the dish
is sold in many of the small
neighborhood delicatessens of
Florence. In the store variety,
dark red wine or *vino nero* is
used instead of the lemon, and a
sprinkling of chopped parsley is
substituted for the onions. This is
a dish for springtime, when fresh
anchovies are available at local
Chinese fish markets. If anchovies are not available, you can
use fresh herring.

2 1/2 pounds (1.25 kg) fresh
    anchovies
2 cups (500 ml) red wine vinegar
1 cup (250 ml) fresh lemon juice
    (about 4 lemons)
2 onions, sliced
Olive oil

Wash anchovies and remove
heads, tails, scales and bones.
Put in bowl and add vinegar so
fish are completely covered.
Allow to marinate for 1 1/2 hours.
Drain anchovies and remove skin.
Cut into 2 inch (5 cm) pieces and
set them in clean bowl. Cover
with lemon juice and allow to
marinate for 2 hours. Drain anchovies and place in yet another
clean bowl. Put onion slices over
and cover completely with olive
oil. After 40 minutes at room
temperature fish will be ready to
eat. Leftovers will keep in
covered container in refrigerator
for up to 2 weeks, but be sure
there is enough oil to cover.

Serves 8
Serve with no wine

SCAMPI ALLA VENEZIANA
Prawns Venetian Style

1 pound (500 g) fresh prawns
1 bay leaf
1/2 cup (125 ml) olive oil
2 very fresh lemons, cut into
  wedges

Cook prawns and bay leaf in boiling water for 3 minutes only. Discard bay leaf. Shell and devein prawns, leaving on the tails. Chill. Serving the prawns in a good-looking clear or white bowl nestled in crushed ice makes a nice show at the table. Offer each person their individual small bowl of olive oil and lemon wedges.

Serves 4
Suggested wine: Pinot Bianco,
  Soave, Fiano, Verdicchio

OSTRICHE GRATINATE ALLA LORENA
Oysters Gratinée

This is a very handsome dish; two oysters alone will impress anyone, so don't serve more than two or three per person otherwise you'll ruin his appetite for the rest of the meal. Upon buying the oysters, make sure they are tightly closed or spring closed when you tap them. Otherwise discard them. Refrigerate and do not open them until ready to cook.

8 or 12 fresh oysters in the shell
1/2 cup (125 ml) chopped fresh
  parsley
1 garlic clove, crushed
4 tablespoons (60 ml) canned
  tuna fish
1 1/2 tablespoons (25 ml) corn oil
1 teaspoon (5 ml) chopped capers
2 tablespoons (30 ml) dried
  bread crumbs
1 tablespoon (15 ml) butter
2 lemons, quartered

Brush oysters under cold running water. Hold oyster with kitchen mitt or towel in one hand and pry open by inserting knife between shells. For heaven's sake, be careful! Cut one side under muscle. Cut muscle loose but leave oyster in its half shell with its own juice. Arrange oysters in good-looking baking dish.

In separate bowl mix parsley, garlic, tuna fish, oil and capers. Distribute the mixture over each oyster. Sprinkle with crumbs and dot with butter. Bake uncovered in preheated 425°F (220°C) oven for 15 to 20 minutes or until tops are golden. Bring to table in baking dish. Offer quartered lemons.

Serves 4
Suggested wine: Gavi, Greco di
  Tufo, Regaleali, Verdicchio,
  Corvo Bianco

Riding on a gondola is a gentle way to see Venice. You glide at water level, without disturbing the reflections. You move quietly through the narrow canals and under bridges. The silence is broken now and then at canal crossings by the warning cry of the gondoliers: "Aaahwehrrr!"

Detail of Campanile di Giotto, or Giotto's tower, in the Piazza del Duomo in Florence

CROSTINI DI FEGATINI
Chicken Livers on Toast

La salvia or sage is one of Italy's most loved herbs. *Qualche foglia di salvia,* or "a few leaves of sage," was the musical phrase that appeared in many of the recipes given verbally to me wherever I went. If you can grow your own sage, a hardy, easy plant to grow, you will enjoy it much more than if you have to resort to using it in dry form. But if dry sage is all you have, use about half the amount given for fresh.

6 chicken livers
1 tablespoon (15 ml) olive oil
1 teaspoon (5 ml) wine vinegar
4 tablespoons (60 ml) butter
$1/2$ teaspoon (3 ml) salt
$1/8$ teaspoon (1 ml) freshly
    ground black pepper
1 tablespoon (15 ml) finely
    chopped fresh sage
2 anchovy fillets, chopped
1 teaspoon (5 ml) chopped capers
12 slices toasted french or italian
    bread

In a skillet, cast iron preferably, sauté chicken livers with olive oil, vinegar, half the butter, salt and pepper, until shrinkage has stopped. Remove livers from skillet and chop. In remaining sauce cook sage for 3 minutes. Add livers and cook stirring until mixture becomes a paste. Add anchovy fillets and capers and cook for another 2 minutes. Remove from heat and add remaining butter. Distribute over bread slices while still hot and serve immediately.

Serves 6
Suggested wine: Soave, Lambrusco Dry, Pomino, Orvieto

BAGNA CAUDA
Piedmontese Hot Dip (Literally, Hot Bath)

As you note, heading the list of ingredients is 1¹/2 heads of garlic. The Italians have an idiom, *mangiar l'aglio,* which literally translates "to eat garlic," but really means "to fume or rage in silence," which is certainly not what a group of Italians does when eating a *bagna cauda.*

This recipe is Gloria Bussa's, whose family has lived in Piemonte for generations. As Gloria says, when hungry *piemontese* get together and it's cold outside, there is bound to be a *bagna cauda* inside. You should try other tender vegetables, and if you want an entirely vegetarian *bagna cauda,* omit the meat.

1¹/2 heads garlic, separated into cloves
Milk as required
3 cans anchovy fillets
2 cups (500 ml) olive oil
¹/4 pound (125 g) butter
2 pounds (1 kg) round steak
³/4 pound (325 g) fresh mushrooms
1 head cabbage
1 cauliflower
1 bell pepper
Juice of 1 lemon
2 loaves sliced french or italian bread

Place individual cloves of garlic with skins on, in small saucepan. Add enough milk to cover and boil 20 minutes. Meanwhile, prepare round steak by cutting into bite-sized pieces. Wash all vegetables, cut them into bite-sized pieces and rinse in cold water acidulated with lemon juice (keeps vegetables from darkening).

Rinse garlic and peel. Discard peels and milk. Mash garlic and anchovies and put in saucepan with olive oil. Simmer, but do not boil, for 5 minutes. Add butter. As soon as butter has melted pour mixture into a chafing dish that will keep it gently simmering but never boiling, because if the garlic burns the whole thing is ruined.

At the table each person will cook the meat and vegetables to individual taste in the chafing dish. Using slices of bread under the tidbit on its trip from dish to mouth will keep the *bagna cauda* from dripping on the tablecloth.

Serves 6
Suggested wine: Soave, Frascati, Pinot Grigio, Corvo Bianco

FONDUTA PIEMONTESE
Piedmontese Fondue

This is a typical dish from Torino in Piemonte. I dare include the truffle in the recipe in the hope that the French, who have succeeded in cultivating this underground fungus delicacy in small amounts, will succeed in cultivating it in enormous quantities so that the cost is brought down to more appetizing levels.

1 pound (450 g) Italian fontina
   cheese
1¹/₃ cups (325 ml) milk
5 egg yolks, beaten
4 tablespoons (60 g) butter
Freshly ground white pepper to
   taste
1 truffle (optional)
12 slices toast, cut into strips

Remove rind from cheese. Cut cheese into cubes. Put in bowl and cover with milk. Allow to rest for 3 to 4 hours, or overnight in refrigerator. In top of double boiler put milk and cheese, making sure the water in the lower pan is hot but not boiling. With wood spoon start stirring, always in the same direction, until the cheese is melted. Mix a tablespoon of sauce with egg yolks and then add yolks a little at a time to the sauce, then add butter. Continue stirring until the *fonduta* is smooth and creamy. Serve in heated deep bowl, sprinkled with pepper and garnished with paper-thin slices of truffle. Serve the strips of toast for dipping into *fonduta*.

Serves 6
Suggested wine: Soave, Gavi,
*   Verdicchio, Torgiano Bianco*

CRESCENTINE BOLOGNESE
Crescents Bologna Style

Crescentine are served during *feste,* or parties, accompanying plates of sliced ham, salami, cheeses and prosciutto, the delicate Italian ham that tastes like the fresh mountain air in which it is hung to dry.

³/4 cup (175 ml) milk
1 tablespoon (15 ml) active dry
   yeast
¹/2 teaspoon (3 ml) salt
2 cups (500 ml) flour
1 tablespoon (15 ml) butter
Cold-pressed sesame oil or corn
   oil, for deep frying
Sliced ham, salami, cheese and
   prosciutto

Heat milk to warm temperature, approximately 110°F (50°C). In bowl dissolve yeast in warm milk. In separate bowl mix salt, flour and butter, working with fingers. Add milk-yeast mixture. Mix and add only enough flour so you end up with a smooth, pliable dough, as for bread. On floured board knead well until dough is not sticky anymore. Make a ball and place in well-oiled bowl. Cover with damp cloth and allow to rise in warm place with no drafts until double in bulk. In deep frying pan heat oil. On floured board roll dough thin and cut into half circles. Fry in hot oil, turning once, until puffed and just light gold. Drain on absorbent paper. At table each person will select what to put on his *crescentine* from the dishes of ham, salami, cheeses or prosciutto.

Serves 6
Suggested wine: Lambrusco,
*   Frascati, Vernaccia di San*
*   Gimignano*

*Twelfth-century Romanesque colon-
nade in the Cloister of Santo
Stefano, Bologna*

PRIMI PIATTI
First Courses

Italians do not serve their pasta as part of their main meat course but serve it as a first course after the antipasto. First courses come in the form of *zuppe* or soups, *risotti* or rice dishes, *paste in brodo,* plain or stuffed noodles in broth and *paste asciutte* or "dry" pasta, so called because it is served with a sauce and not in broth. *Gnocchi* and *polenta* fall within this category as well. *Gnocchi* are dumplings made of flour with the addition of potatoes or cream of wheat, *polenta,* cheese and so on. *Polenta* or cornmeal is made from maize which in Italy is known as *gran-turco.* Some say this name was given to maize because it first came to Italy via Turkey to Venice. Others maintain that even though maize originated in the American continent, all things foreign, including corn, were labeled Turkish or Saracen by the fifteenth-century Italians. And, so they say, *grano turco* or Turkish grain, stuck to this day.

WINES AND FIRST COURSES

With some exceptions, I would advise serving the same wine with the first course as has been served with the antipasto. In case no antipasto is served, I would normally suggest a dry white wine as the proper accompaniment to a first course. With broths, it is best to serve no wine at all, but should one wish to present a wine with this course, I would suggest a good Sardinian Vernaccia or a very dry Marsala. For treatment of wines see page 9.

One of the heads girding the capital of a column in the lower arcade of the Ducal Palace in Venice. The patina of salt air and time gives these sculptures an air of mystery impossible to fully capture in a sketch.

Zuppe e Brodi
Soups and Broths

BRODO
Broth or Stock

Italians seldom add plain water as the liquid during cooking, they add *brodo* or broth instead. The basics for making *brodo* are meat, vegetables, seasoning and water. For meat you can use what is available such as meat, bones, chicken skins, and for certain dishes, fish or fish heads. If you are short of time, you can substitute commercial stock base or bouillion cubes diluted with boiling water.

BRODO DI MANZO
Beef Broth

1 1/2 pounds (750 g) lean beef
1 or 2 pieces beef bones
1 teaspoon (5 ml) salt
1/2 teaspoon (2 ml) freshly
   ground black pepper
2 quarts (2 L) water
1 small onion
1 carrot
1 celery stalk
2 parsley sprigs
1 leek (optional)
1 egg white (for clearing broth)

Wash meat and bones. Put in large pot with salt, pepper and water to cover. Bring to boil. Lower heat and simmer for 2 hours. Skim off foam from top. Add vegetables and continue simmering, partly covered, for 1 more hour. Pass broth through colander, reserving meat and vegetables for other dishes (stew, minestrone, cream soup). Refrigerate until fat solidifies on surface. Remove fat and discard. If you want a clear broth add raw egg white to the strained broth and bring to boil while beating with wire whisk. Cover and simmer 20 minutes. Pass through colander lined with clean damp cloth. Broth may be refrigerated in covered container for later use.

Makes 1 1/2 quarts (1.5 L) broth

Cosmati *work, or inlay of colored stones, pulpit of San Miniato al Monte, eleventh and twelfth centuries. San Miniato is one of the loveliest examples of Romanesque architecture in Florence.*

BRODO DI POLLO
Chicken Broth

4 pounds (2 kg) chicken parts,
    except liver
2 quarts (2 L) water
1 teaspoon (5 ml) salt
1/2 teaspoon (2 ml) freshly
    ground black pepper
1 small onion
1 carrot
1 celery stalk
2 parsley sprigs
1 leek (optional)

Follow the same procedure as for
brodo di manzo, beef broth,
preceding.

Makes 1 1/2 quarts (1.5 L) broth.

PASTA IN BRODO
Pasta in Broth

To preceding recipes for beef or
chicken broth add *tortellini,* page
47, *cappelletti,* page 44, or other
small pasta.

ZUPPA PAVESE
Soup Pavia Style

8 thick slices french or italian
    bread
4 tablespoons (60 ml) butter
8 eggs
4 tablespoons (60 ml) freshly
    grated parmesan cheese
1 1/2 quarts (1.5 L) boiling beef
    broth, page 30

Fry bread in melted butter until
golden on each side. Put 2 slices
in each heated individual soup
bowl. Break one egg over each
bread slice. If a firmer egg is
preferred, poach eggs before
placing on bread. Sprinkle
parmesan cheese over all. While
broth keeps boiling, ladle it into
each bowl, very gently so as not
to break up eggs. Serve immediately.

Serves 4
Serve with no wine

STRACCIATELLA
ARMANDO
"Little Rags" Soup

1 quart (1 L) chicken broth,
    preceding
3 eggs
3 tablespoons (45 ml) freshly
    grated parmesan cheese
2 tablespoons (30 ml) dried
    bread crumbs
1 tablespoon (15 ml) finely
    chopped fresh parsley
1/4 teaspoon (1 ml) freshly
    grated nutmeg
1 tablespoon (15 ml) cold water

Salt and freshly ground black
    pepper to taste
Freshly grated parmesan cheese
1 lemon, cut into wedges

In soup pot heat broth. In the
meantime beat eggs with all
other ingredients. When broth
boils, lower heat and pour egg
mixture into broth. Stir gently.
Offer a side bowl of parmesan
cheese and a plate of lemon
wedges.

Serves 4
Serve with no wine

MINESTRONE ALLA
GENOVESE
Vegetable Soup Genoa Style

Minestrone varies according to
the area where it is made and
also according to what vegetables
are in season. What makes a
minestrone *genovese* is the addition of the famous *pesto,* the
aromatic sweet basil sauce ground
in a mortar. Many Italians like to
serve minestrone in a soup tureen
over day-old crusty italian or
french bread laid at bottom of
the tureen. If you do that, omit
the pasta. Leftovers should be
stored without the bread, in the
refrigerator.

1/2 cup (125 ml) dried white
    or kidney beans

2 tablespoons (30 ml) olive oil
1 onion, coarsely chopped
1 garlic clove, crushed
2 quarts (2 L) beef broth,
    page 30
2 potatoes, peeled and diced
2 carrots, sliced
3 celery stalks, sliced
Salt and freshly ground black
    pepper to taste
1/2 cup (125 ml) fresh peas
1 cup (250 ml) *ditalini* or other
    short pasta tubes
1 1/2 tablespoons (25 ml) *pesto
per minestrone,* following
Freshly grated parmesan cheese

Wash and soak beans overnight
in water to cover. In large pan
put olive oil, onion and garlic
and sauté but do not allow to
brown. Add beans with their
water plus the broth. Bring to
boil, lower heat and simmer for 1
hour or until beans are tender.
Add potatoes, carrots and celery
to pot. Season with salt and pepper and continue simmering 10
minutes or until vegetables are
almost cooked. Add peas and
ditalini; cook for another 8
minutes. Mix the *pesto* with a
cup of the soup and add to pot.
Turn heat off and serve in 2 or 3
minutes. Offer freshly grated parmesan cheese for those who are
partial to it.

Serves 6
Serve with no wine

*Salvaged building panel laid to rest
in the courtyard garden of the Palazzo Reale on Via Balbi, Genova*

PESTO PER MINESTRONE ALLA GENOVESE
Genoese Green Sauce for
Minestrone Soup

1/2 cup (125 ml) fresh sweet basil
    leaves
1 parsley sprig
1 garlic clove
2 teaspoons (10 ml) pine nuts
1/4 cup (50 ml) freshly grated
    parmesan cheese
1 tablespoon (15 ml) butter
1 tablespoon (15 ml) olive oil

With mortar and pestle grind all
ingredients to a smooth paste.

MINESTRONE PASSATO
Strained Vegetable Soup

Follow preceding recipe for *minestrone alla genovese* until the
vegetables are cooked. Pass contents of pot through sieve. Return to pot, and when hot add
ditalini or other small noodles.
When noodles are done add the
1 1/2 tablespoons (25 ml) *pesto.*
Turn heat off and serve in 2 or 3
minutes.

Serves 6
Serve with no wine

CARABACCIA
Onion Soup

Carabaccia or *zuppa di cipolle* is
said to have been born in
Florence. I suppose someone
should let the French know that.

1/2 pound (250 g) white
    onions, thinly sliced
4 tablespoons (60 ml) butter
1 1/2 tablespoons (25 ml) flour
1 quart (1 L) beef broth, page 30
1/4 teaspoon (1 ml) freshly
    ground white pepper
3/4 cup (175 ml) shredded
    gruyère cheese
1/4 cup (50 ml) freshly grated
    parmesan cheese
8 slices french or italian bread,
    toasted

In soup pot sauté onions in
melted butter until golden but
not brown. Add flour, cooking
until flour is barely brown. Add
broth and pepper (salt is not
needed). Simmer 15 minutes. In
heated soup tureen or heated individual soup bowls, cover bottom with toasted bread, sprinkle
with cheeses and gently pour
soup over. Serve piping hot.

Serves 4
Suggested wine: Corvo Bianco,
    Orvieto

ACQUA COTTA
Tuscan Pepper and Tomato Soup
(Literally, Cooked Water)

1/4 cup (50 ml) olive oil
4 tablespoons (60 ml) butter
2 large onions, chopped
2 celery stalks, sliced
1 large bell pepper, cored and
    sliced
3 large tomatoes, peeled, seeded
    and chopped, or 16-ounce (450
    g) can tomatoes
Salt and freshly ground black
    pepper to taste
2 quarts (2 L) boiling water
4 eggs, beaten
1 cup (250 ml) freshly grated
    parmesan cheese
12 slices toasted french or italian
    bread

In large casserole put oil, butter,
onions and celery, and sauté until limp but not brown. Add bell
pepper and tomatoes and simmer
20 minutes Add boiling water,
salt sparingly, and pepper to
taste. Simmer 10 minutes. Mix
beaten eggs with cheese and add
to soup. Stir, removing pot immediately from heat. In each
prewarmed serving bowl place 2
slices toast and cover with hot
soup.

Serves 8
Serve with no wine

Tartaruga, *turtle. Detail from bronze doors of the Cathedral in Pisa, facing the Baptistry.*

ZUPPA DI FAGIOLI ALLA TOSCANA
Tuscan Bean Soup

$1/2$ pound (250 g) small dried
   white beans
2 tablespoons (30 ml) olive oil
1 garlic clove, crushed
1 tablespoon (15 ml) freshly
   chopped parsley
1 celery stalk, finely chopped
$1/4$ teaspoon (2 ml) freshly
   ground black pepper
2 quarts (2 L) water
1 cup (250 ml) tomato sauce,
   page 62 (optional)
1 teaspoon (5 ml) salt

Wash and soak beans overnight.
In large casserole put oil, garlic,
parsley, celery and pepper and
sauté until barely brown. Add
beans, water, tomato sauce (if
desired) and salt. Bring to boil,
lower temperature and simmer
until beans are tender, about 2
hours. Remove half of beans and
puree by passing through sieve or
in blender. Return mashed beans
to pot; add salt and pepper if
needed.

Serves 6
Suggested wine: Chianti, Barbera

PASTA E FASOI
Venetian Bean and Noodle Soup

1 1/2 cups (375 ml) dried white or
    red beans
1 tablespoon (15 ml) olive oil
1 garlic clove
4 ounces (100 g) pork skin or
    thick bacon or ham bone
1/2 onion, finely chopped
1 celery stalk, finely chopped
1/2 carrot, finely chopped
1 tomato with skin and seeds re-
    moved, or 1 cup (250 ml)
    tomato sauce, page 62
1/4 teaspoon (2 ml) freshly
    ground black pepper
2 beef bouillon cubes
1 parsley sprig, finely chopped
3 leaves sweet basil, chopped, or
    1/4 teaspoon (2 ml) dried
    basil
1/2 pound (250 g) noodles
2 tablespoons (30 ml) olive oil
Plenty of freshly grated parmesan
    cheese

Wash beans and soak in cold
water overnight or 8 hours. In
casserole with 1 tablespoon (15
ml) olive oil, sauté garlic clove
until pale gold, not brown.

Remove and discard garlic. Add
pork skin or substitute, beans
and their water, vegetables, pepper, bouillon cubes, parsley and
basil. Add 2 quarts (2 L) water.
Bring to boil, lower heat and
simmer uncovered for 2 hours or
until beans are tender. If cooking
with ham bone, remove and discard. Take half the beans out
and pass through a sieve or mash
in blender. Add mashed beans
back to the pot. Bring to boil,
add noodles and cook until *al
dente,* or a bit firm. Add 2
tablespoons (30 ml) olive oil. Offer parmesan cheese to sprinkle
over.

Serves 6
*Suggested wine: Chianti, Lacrima
    Cristi Rosso, Barbera*

ZUPPA DI PESCE
Fish Soup

Fish soup is eaten throughout
Italy, but each city has its own
particular way to make it and the
fish used depends on what is
locally available. This recipe is
the best I found and comes out
very good using rock cod, had-

dock, catfish, sea bass or
mackerel. I have tried it with half
rock cod and half butterfish quite
successfully. Make sure you debone the fish thoroughly. In
order to keep the fish from falling apart during cooking you can
lay the fish over coarse salt for a
while; this hardens the fish.

3 tablespoons (45 ml) olive oil
1 garlic clove, chopped
1 medium onion, chopped
4 parsley sprigs, chopped
2 cups (500 ml) cold water
1 1/2 pounds (750 g) white fish,
    deboned and cut in pieces
Salt and freshly ground black
    pepper to taste

In heavy pot or casserole put oil,
garlic, onion and parsley and
sauté for 10 minutes. Add water,
fish, salt and pepper. Bring to
boil, lower heat, cover and simmer 10 minutes, until fish is just
done. Serve hot with hardy bread
and butter.

Serves 4
*Suggested wine: Verdicchio,
    Frascati, Elba Bianco, or wine
    served with antipasto*

Detail on a pillar at the entry to the Baptistry in Pisa. It depicts the harvesting of grain with a sickle, which my friend Paul Meserve, who spent many years in Italy, says represents fertility.

Paste e Salse
Noodles and Sauces

Italians are so imaginative and versatile in their handling of pasta that they are naively identified throughout the world with noodles, as if that were all they make. In reality even though pasta is a staple, it does not constitute the main dish of the meal, and is generally served in small portions.

Northern Italy, like its French neighbor, is masterful in the creation of different sauces. Subtle and delicate concoctions are their sauces, differing from the spicier flavors of their brothers to the south.

The sauces included in this section are those that are used mainly with pasta. A complete list of the sauces in this book is given in the index.

Pasta should always be cooked in plenty of salted boiling water. Use at least two quarts (2 L) water for one-half pound (250 g) noodles so that pasta will not be crowded.

PASTA DELLA NONNA
Grandma's Noodle Dough

This is a very basic recipe. It can be used for pasta envelopes to be stuffed or for noodles. If you are going to stuff you should work in a cool place away from drafts so your dough does not dry up. If the dough should dry before you close the noodle bags, you can dampen the edges of the dough so they will stick together and hold in the stuffing. If you are making plain noodles you can cut them and, while dough is still fresh, cook in plenty of boiling salted water. Or you can cut them, give them the shapes you want and allow to dry: When thoroughly dry you can store noodles in tightly covered containers, in a cool place, for future use.

3 cups (700 ml) flour
4 eggs
1/2 teaspoon (2 ml) salt

Sift flour on marble or wood board. Make crater in center. Add eggs and salt. Work together to make a firm but not crumbly dough. Knead vigorously until pliable and elastic. Make ball and allow to rest 10 minutes covered with cloth. On floured tablecloth roll dough very thin. Cut, shape, stuff as desired. Cook in boiling salted water until just firm or *al dente*. Drain and serve with one of the many sauces included here or simply with melted butter and freshly grated parmesan cheese.

Serves 4 if plain noodles, 6 if in broth or stuffed
Suggested wine: According to the sauce served

Detail of brickwork on the Church of Calvary at the Seven Churches of Santo Stefano in Bologna

TAGLIATELLE CON RAGÙ ALLA EGNI
Long Flat Noodles with Meat Sauce

To think of Armando's Restaurant in Florence is to think of Egni. Egni brings you your food quickly, piping hot when it's meant to be and never before you are ready for it. But if you go there, don't ask Egni for coffee at the end of the meal. We habitually did, and eventually wondered why it took a good ten minutes before it arrived, and was always cold. Enlightenment came when we discovered that Egni would, uncomplainingly, abandon the restaurant for the corner bar, and buy our coffee to go!

In Italy, restaurants are meant for eating and, of course, the companionable wine. Sipping Italian coffee is an activity that is classified with "having a drink" at that venerable institution, the bar, which serves liquor, a glass of wine, coffee, pastry, sandwiches and ice cream, and sells cigarettes and the like. The atmosphere is light, friendly, and minors are not prohibited. Coffee drinking is something you do any time of the day, and the coffee may be spiked, topped with whipped cream, sweet or bitter, but always strong. The American watered-down version is referred to as *caffè brutto,* or ugly coffee.

Egni's recipes for *ragù* and *tagliatelle* follow.

RAGÙ ALLA EGNI
Bolognese Meat Sauce

1 small onion
1 celery stalk
1 carrot
2 sprigs parsley
3 tablespoons (45 ml) butter
1 tablespoon (15 ml) olive oil
1 pound (500 g) lean ground
    round
2 cups (500 ml) tomato sauce,
    page 62
Salt and freshly ground black
    pepper to taste

Chop onion, celery, carrot and parsley *finissimo* or *fino fino* as Italians say for very fine. In oil and butter sauté vegetables until they start to get gold but not brown. Add meat and with fork or spoon work meat and vegetables into a fine even texture without large pieces of meat. Keep sautéeing until meat is cooked but not browned. Add tomato sauce, salt and pepper. Lower temperature to medium and allow to simmer another 15 minutes turning once in a while. Egni advised this short cooking of the sauce because he said *non dovete cucinare a morte i pomodori,* you don't want to cook the tomato to death. Serve on homemade *tagliatelle,* following, or other noodles and offer freshly grated parmesan cheese.

Serves 4 to 6
Suggested wine: Grignolino, San
   Giovese, Valpolicella

TAGLIATELLE
Long Flat Noodles

3 cups (700 ml) flour
4 eggs

Mix flour and eggs and knead until you have firm, pliable, non-sticky dough, about 15 minutes. On floured tablecloth or board roll into very thin, large rectangle. Let rest a few minutes. Dust top with flour and fold over one edge about 3 fingers wide. Keep folding over until you have a flat roll. With sharp knife cut into slices about 1/4 inch (6 mm) wide. Unroll and separate them on floured tablecloth and let them dry a few minutes or longer. Cook in plenty of boiling salted water until *al dente* still firm. Serve with a dollop of *ragù,* preceding, and offer plenty of freshly grated parmesan cheese.

Serves 4
Suggested wine: Grignolino, San
   Giovese, Valpolicella

SUGO PER PASTA DI MADDALENA
Spaghetti Sauce with Giblets

I can't resist the temptation to give you the recipe in the gargantuan scale it was given to me. If you give a large dinner party you'll be ready for it. Otherwise put whatever you can't eat at one sitting into freezer containers for future use.

$1/4$ cup (50 ml) olive oil
2 large onions, chopped
3 pounds (1.5 kg) lean ground beef
3 pounds (1.5 kg) chicken hearts and gizzards, chopped
$1^{1}/2$ tablespoons (25 ml) salt
2 teaspoons (10 ml) freshly ground black pepper
1 teaspoon (5 ml) ground allspice
6 slices dried mushrooms, chopped
1 celery stalk, chopped
2 garlic cloves, crushed
5 parsley sprigs, chopped
1 teaspoon (5 ml) dried sweet basil or a handful fresh basil leaves, chopped
2 carrots, chopped
1 fresh rosemary sprig, or $1/2$ teaspoon (3 ml) dried rosemary
1 teaspoon (5 ml) dried thyme, or 2 teaspoons (10 ml) chopped fresh thyme
3 16-ounce (450 g) cans tomato puree
3 cups (750 ml) water
3 mild italian sausages, cut in pieces

In large heavy pot heat olive oil. Add onions and sautè until soft. Add ground beef, chicken hearts and gizzards and sautè until well browned. Add salt, pepper, allspice, mushrooms, celery, garlic, parsley, sweet basil, carrot, rosemary and thyme. Stir well and cook 5 minutes. Add tomato puree and water. Bring to boil, lower heat and simmer uncovered for 2 hours. Add sausage, stir well and cook a final 10 minutes.

Serves 30
Suggested wine: Valpolicella, Chianti

PESTO ALLA GENOVESE
Genoese Green Sauce

Basilico genovese, or Genoese basil, is said to be the best in all of Italy, and its superior quality is attributed to the pure water and fresh air of the region. It is said that people who know can smell the difference between the *basilico* grown in Genoa and that grown elsewhere.

Even though this delightful sauce is native to Genova it is loved throughout Italy. You will find it everywhere served over pasta or included in minestrone. *Pesto alla genovese* may be served on lasagne, *gnocchi di patate,* or noodles with lots of parmesan cheese. If you are using commercial noodles instead of home-made, use the old Italian artifice of cooking the noodles with a potato cut up in small pieces, draining when done and serving the potato mixed with the noodles before adding the sauce on top. The pasta will be almost like homemade, a bit more starchy and not so precise looking as commercial noodles.

1 cup (250 ml) fresh sweet basil
  leaves
1 parsley sprig
2 garlic cloves
1^1/$_2$ tablespoons (25 ml) pine nuts
^{1}/$_4$ cup (50 ml) freshly grated
  pecorino cheese or other
  piquant salty cheese
^{1}/$_4$ cup (50 ml) freshly grated
  parmesan cheese
1 cup (250 ml) olive oil (approximately)

In a mortar put basil, parsley,
garlic and pine nuts. With pestle
grind contents of mortar to a
paste. Add cheeses and continue
grinding. Add enough oil to
make a dense, well amalgamated
sauce. Though some add salt to
the sauce, I have found that the
cheeses have enough.

Serves 4
*Suggested wine for pasta with
  pesto alla genovese: Soave,
  Pinot Bianco, Corvo Bianco, or
  wine served with antipasto*

*Detail of pregnant women at the
left of the main portals of the Cattedrale di San Lorenzo, Genova*

CAPPELLETTI
Little Hats

Cappelletti are so named because they come out looking like little hats. They come from Emilia-Romagna, the area where you find Parma, home of parmesan cheese; Ferrara, known for its flour; and Bologna, the city of towers and *ragù*, the famous meat sauce loved in all of Italy. *Cappelletti* are eaten with butter and plenty of parmesan chese, or with *ragù*. They are eaten with cream sauces or *in brodo*, cooked in boiling clear broth, and served as a soup (in which case they are made smaller).

THE FILLING
1/2 chicken breast, or
   1 lean pork chop
2 tablespoons (30 ml) butter
1/2 pound (225 g) ricotta cheese
1/2 cup (125 ml) freshly grated
   parmesan cheese
1 egg and 1 egg yolk
Salt and freshly ground white
   pepper to taste
1 pinch freshly grated nutmeg
Grated rind of 1/2 lemon

THE DOUGH
2 cups (500 ml) flour
2 eggs
1 egg white, if needed

To make the filling, sauté breast of chicken or pork chop in butter and chop very finely. In bowl mix chopped meat with ricotta cheese, parmesan, egg and yolk, salt, pepper, nutmeg and lemon rind. Refrigerate until ready to use.

Make the dough by mixing flour and eggs, using the extra white only as needed to make a firm, pliable, non-sticky dough. Knead until smooth, about 10 minutes. Make into a ball and allow to rest covered with cloth for 10 minutes. On floured surface (be it wood, tablecloth or best of all marble) extend dough with rolling pin until very thin. Cut into circles 2½ inches (6 cm) in diameter. Put a little filling in center of each circle and fold in half, pinching edges to seal together. If dough is a bit too

dry to seal properly, dampen edges with wet finger before folding. Put one finger over the half circle you have just made and bring ends over the finger, overlap, press them together and turn them up, to complete the "brim" of the hat. Leave the finished *cappelletti* on a floured cloth to dry before cooking. Cook in plenty of boiling broth, like the people in Romagna do, or in boiling salted water, until done, about 5 minutes. Drain and serve with sauce or serve in its broth as soup.

Serves 4 to 6
Suggested wine: Trebbiano, Lambrusco Dry, Corvo Bianco

GNOCCHI VERDI CON SALSA D'AGLIO
Green Dumplings with Garlic Sauce

I GNOCCHI
1 pound (500 g) fresh spinach
½ pound (250 g) ricotta cheese
2 eggs
1½ cups (375 ml) flour
1 teaspoon (5 ml) salt
⅛ teaspoon (1 ml) freshly
    ground white pepper (optional)
¼ teaspoon (2 ml) freshly grated
    nutmeg
2 tablespoons (30 ml) freshly
    grated parmesan cheese

THE GARLIC SAUCE
4 tablespoons (60 ml) butter
1 large garlic clove, crushed

Plenty of freshly grated parmesan at table

To make the *gnocchi*, wash and drain spinach. Cook in covered pan without adding water, for 5 minutes. Pass through a colander or mash in blender. Put mashed spinach in large bowl. Add all other ingredients, except those for the garlic sauce. Mix well. Dough will be sticky, but don't worry. On well-floured board shape dough into long, finger-thick ropes. Cut ropes into 1 inch (3 cm) lengths. Cook them in plenty of boiling salted water until they float.

In the meantime put butter and garlic in small saucepan and sauté until garlic is light gold but not brown, otherwise *porta l'amaro,* or the garlic becomes bitter. Remove and discard garlic.

When *gnocchi* float, take them out, gently, with slotted spoon and put into heated serving dish. Add garlic sauce and serve. Put bowls of parmesan cheese where everybody can get at them.

Serves 4
Suggested wine: Verdicchio, Corvo Bianco, Orvieto, Torgiano

GNOCCHI DI GLORIA
Potato Dumplings

2 pounds (1 kg) potatoes
2 cups (500 ml) flour
2 egg yolks
1 teaspoon (5 ml) salt
2 tablespoons (30 ml) corn oil

Ragù, page 41
Freshly grated parmesan cheese

Boil potatoes in their jackets, peel and pass through sieve. Add flour, egg yolks, salt and oil. Work together until you have a soft but consistent dough. On floured board make long finger-thick ropes and cut in small pieces. Shape them into textured little "shells" by pressing them with a rolling motion on inside surface of rounded colander or fork. Put a bunch of *gnocchi* into plenty of boiling salted water. When water starts to boil again, they are ready. Take them out carefully with slotted spoon. Serve in heated platter with *ragù* and plenty of freshly grated parmesan cheese.

Serves 4
Suggested wine: Grignolino, Sangiovese, Valpolicella

The Tetrarchs, a fourth-century Byzantine work done in red porphyry, in a corner of San Marco in Venice, near the Ducal Palace. The interesting way the Venetians installed the two groups of two gives them a sense of motion, a dimension beyond sculpture.

GNOCCHI DI POVERI
Poor Man's Dumplings

This recipe comes from Signora Venturi Secondo on the lovely island of Elba. It was on Elba that Napoleon was held a prisoner and from where he escaped to fight and lose the battle of Waterloo. For a less ambitious person, Elba is perfect with its warm beaches, clear seas and Aleatico, a deliciously piquant after-dinner wine.

2 pounds (1 kg) potatoes
1 1/2 cups (375 ml) flour
3/4 teaspoon (4 ml) salt
Ragù, page 41, or melted butter and crushed sage, or butter and parmesan cheese

Boil potatoes with skins on. Peel and pass through sieve. While still warm, add flour and salt. Work all together until you have a soft but consistent dough. On lightly floured board make long (finger-thick) ropes. Cut ropes in small pieces and shape them into textured little "shells" by pressing them with a rolling motion on inside surface of a colander or fork dusted with flour. Cook *gnocchi* in boiling salted water until they float. Drain and serve with *ragù* or with melted butter and a bit of crushed fresh sage, as they do in Bergamo, or simply with butter and a sprinkling of parmesan cheese.

Serves 4
Suggested wine: Elba Bianco, Pomino, Orvieto

TORTELLINI
Stuffed Noodles

Tortellini may be served in two ways, *pasta in brodo* (noodles in broth) and *pasta asciutta* ("dry" pasta because the noodles are not in broth). For the *brodo* in *tortellini in brodo* see page 30 for beef broth and see page 32 for chicken broth. For the *ragù* in *tortellini in ragù* see page 41. *Tortellini* can be served with only melted butter and parmesan cheese and still be delicious. And uncooked *tortellini* can be stored in boxes in your freezer for later use.

THE DOUGH
2 cups (500 ml) flour
2 eggs

Put flour on wood board and hollow a crater in center. Put eggs in center and work with fingers to make firm dough. Knead until elastic and non-sticky. Make a ball and allow to rest, covered with cloth, for 15 minutes.

THE STUFFING
1 pound (500 g) fresh spinach
1 pound (500 g) ricotta cheese
1/4 pound (125 g) parmesan cheese, freshly grated
Salt to taste
2 eggs
1/4 teaspoon (1 ml) freshly grated nutmeg

Wash spinach in cold water. Drain and cook a few minutes in covered pot with only the water that clings to leaves. Drain, squeeze dry and chop very fine. Pass ricotta through a sieve into a bowl. Add spinach, parmesan, salt, eggs and nutmeg.

MAKING THE TORTELLINI

On floured board roll dough thinly flat. Cut into circles with rim of small glass dipped in flour. Put a little filling in center of each circle. Fold in half pressing edges together to seal in stuffing. Join the two ends and press them together. Lay *tortellini* on floured cloth to dry or cook right away in large pot of boiling salted water. When they float they are ready. Drain and serve immediately.

Serves 4
Suggested wine: According to the sauce served

AGNOLLOTTI DI PATATE
Noodles Stuffed with Potatoes

After all the months of gathering recipes, I looked forward to a relaxed conclusion of rest, snorkeling and fishing on the island of Elba. You can imagine my surprise when I found myself in another kitchen, elbow deep in flour with Carmela, making pasta.

Carmela runs the kitchen at Villa Miramare. Her powerful arms handle the dough like a karate fighter. She beats the dough and whips the table with it rythmically and noisily. But when the time comes to shape the *agnollotti* her fingers become the delicate tools of a jeweler.

To make *agnollotti,* you need old potatoes, Carmela says, because they are more albuminous and hold together with less flour. She makes the *agnollotti* two ways. One is like the *Piacenza ravioli:* by making wide ribbons of pasta with her noodle-making machine, putting the filling on the ribbons, evenly spaced, about 1^1/$_2$ inches (4.5 cm) apart and covering with another ribbon of pasta. She then presses around each little hump to seal, and cuts with a round pastry cutter. The other way she makes these little morsels is the *sardi,* or Sardinian, manner of her ancestors. To believe this phenomenon you have to see it done. She extends the dough on a floured tablecloth, cuts circles, places a small gob of filling in center of each circle. And then instead of folding over and pinching the edges sealed, which is run of the mill, she holds the circle with stuffing in her cupped left hand and with her right she begins literally to zip up the dough by alternating thumb and forefinger while pushing the edge of the dough inwards. What comes out is a neat lozenge with a zipper along its length. When I watched her make it, I was incredulous, so I marveled, "Carmela, *che bello!* (how beautiful!) But will they hold the stuffing in?" She simply smirked with her usual condescension, and they did.

THE STUFFING
4 pounds (2 kg) potatoes
4 garlic cloves, crushed
Handful fresh mint leaves
^{1}/$_4$ pound (125 g) *formaggio misto* or mixed grated cheeses: parmesan, mozzarella and pecorino or other
^{1}/$_4$ pound (125 g) butter
^{1}/$_4$ cup (50 ml) olive oil
Salt and freshly ground black pepper to taste

THE DOUGH
4 cups (1 L) flour
Water
Salt
Butter and freshly grated parmesan cheese, or *ragù,* page 41

To make the stuffing, boil potatoes with skins. Peel and mash. With mortar and pestle mash garlic and mint leaves. Add mixed cheeses, butter and oil; keep mashing until smooth. Add contents of mortar to potatoes. Add salt and pepper to taste. When you are finished mixing, the tops of potatoes should be oily.

To make the dough, put flour on marble table or wood board. Make a crater in the center and add slightly salted water as needed to incorporate all the flour and make a stiff but not dry dough. Work well for 5 minutes or until not sticky anymore. If you will be using a noodle-making machine to make the pasta you can stop kneading now, otherwise continue working the dough until very elastic and pliable, about 10 minutes more. Now you are ready to form the *agnollotti*. In the beginning I described to you the ways Carmela shapes *agnollotti,* which you can follow. Otherwise, on floured tablecloth or board roll the dough very thin. Put small gobs of potato filling over half the surface about 1^1/$_2$ inches (4 cm) apart. Gently, fold dough over in half to cover gobs. Press around each gob to seal both layers of dough and with pastry cutter cut into circles. Allow to dry for a while on the cloth. Cook small batches of *agnollotti* in boiling salted water until they float. Drain and serve in heated platter with butter and grated parmesan cheese or *ragù*.

Serves 6
Suggested wine: Lambrusco Dry,
  Trebbiano

Detail above the main entrance to the Duomo, or Church of Santa Maria del Fiore, in Florence

RAVIOLI DELLA FAMIGLIA BUSSA
Ravioli of the Bussa Family

When Gloria gave me her *piemontese* family recipe for ravioli there was no question that I was being entrusted with a symbol of family pride. As such I was expected to record it in its entirety, without editorializing. I do so, without regrets; they are simply scrumptuous.

The quantities given make about fifty dozen and since you can't stop eating them before you've gone through a couple dozen, you can count on feeding twenty-four guests and yourself at one sitting. The alternative is to save them in your freezer for a bright future. To freeze uncooked ravioli, place them in a box in alternating layers between sheets of wax paper, dusting with flour under and over each layer. To cook frozen ravioli drop them without thawing into rapidly boiling salted water and cook until they float to the top. Serve the same way you would the freshly made ravioli in this recipe.

ON THE FIRST DAY

IL PIENO

THE FILLING

2 pounds (1 kg) pork roast (any kind), cut up
Salt and freshly ground black pepper
2 celery stalks
1 fresh sage sprig, or 1 teaspoon (5 ml) dried sage
3 garlic cloves
1 cup (250 ml) water
3 pounds (1.5 kg) beef roast or stewing beef, cut up
1 fresh rosemary sprig, or 1 teaspoon (5 ml) dried rosemary
1 fresh oregano sprig, or 1 teaspoon (5 ml) dried oregano
1 1/2 pounds (750 g) rabbit or chicken, cut up
A few chive leaves
1 medium onion
1 beef brain
2 mild italian sausages
2 1/2 pounds (1.25 kg) spinach, cooked and well drained
12 eggs
1 cup (250 ml) freshly grated parmesan cheese
3/4 cup (175 ml) dried bread crumbs

In lightly greased pot, brown pork roast, add salt and pepper to taste, 1 celery stalk, sage, 1 garlic clove and a cup of water. Simmer at least 45 minutes, until pork is tender, adding water as needed. Allow to cool. Save drippings for the gravy. Brown beef the same way, add salt and pepper to taste, 1 clove garlic, rosemary, oregano, celery stalk and cook about 45 minutes until done, adding water as needed. Allow to cool. Save drippings for the gravy. In the same manner brown rabbit or chicken. Add 1 cup water, salt and pepper to taste, chives, onion and 1 clove garlic. Cook until done adding water as needed. Allow to cool. Remove bones and save drippings for the gravy. Place beef brain into boiling water to cover. Return to boil and cook 2 minutes. Remove brain to ice water. When cool, peel, discarding skin and blood vessels. Place italian sausage in boiling water; cook 4 minutes. Remove from water and allow to cool. Grind all cooled cooked meat and spinach in meat grinder and mix well in large bowl. Add 4 teaspoons (20 ml) salt, 1 teaspoon (5 ml) freshly ground pepper, eggs, cheese and bread crumbs. Blend thoroughly. By now you and the day are done, so put the filling in refrigerator until tomorrow.

ON SECOND DAY:
LA PASTA
THE DOUGH
6 cups (1.5 L) flour
2 teaspoons (10 ml) salt
1 1/4 cups (300 ml) warm water
5 egg yolks
2 eggs
2 tablespoons (30 ml) corn oil

Put flour on wood board and make well in center. Add remaining ingredients. Mix well. Knead 8 minutes until dough is smooth and shiny using additional flour as needed to prevent sticking. Divide dough into 3 equal parts. Working with one part at a time form into a ball. Flatten ball on lightly floured marble or cloth-covered table to about 1 foot (30 cm) size with palm of hand. Using large rolling pin, roll out dough until it is very thin. This takes some time as eggs tend to contract dough as you flatten it. But eventually you will have a circle about 1 yard (1 meter) in diameter.

PUTTING THE RAVIOLI TOGETHER
Remember the filling? It's taking up half your refrigerator. Using spatula or large knife, spread one third of the filling evenly over half the dough circle, leaving a clear border about a finger wide around the circumference. The filling layer will be about 1/4 inch (0.5 cm) thick. Fold empty half of dough over filling. Using ravioli rolling pin, roll slowly in the direction of the straight side over entire length of dough, applying pressure to seal dough around each *raviolo*. (If you don't have a ravioli rolling pin, press with your fingers, making 1 inch (3 cm) rows across dough in both directions.) With ravioli cutting wheel or kitchen knife, cut along rows to separate ravioli. With spatula or knife, gently lift ravioli and place on floured cloth. Repeat process with other 2 parts of dough and remaining filling.

Cook ravioli by placing 2 dozen per person into plenty of rapidly boiling salted water. Ravioli are done when they float to top. Drain and serve with *il sugo*, the gravy (which is described in the following recipe) and freshly grated parmesan cheese. You can also serve ravioli with other sauces given in this book.

Makes about 50 dozen ravioli, or 25 servings

IL SUGO
THE GRAVY
1/2 pound (250 g) chicken gizzards and hearts
1/2 pound (250 g) lean ground beef
1/3 cup (75 ml) drippings from roast beef or pork
1 tablespoon (15 ml) chopped fresh parsley
1 fresh rosemary sprig or 1/2 teaspoon (2 ml) dry rosemary
1 small onion, chopped
1 tablespoon (15 ml) chopped dried mushrooms
Salt and freshly ground black pepper to taste
1 cup (250 ml) dry white wine
1 mild italian sausage, chopped
Freshly grated parmesan cheese

In saucepan brown chopped gizzards, hearts and ground beef in drippings from roast meat. Add parsley, rosemary, onion, mushrooms, salt and pepper. Cook 5 minutes. Add wine and simmer 45 minutes. Add sausage and cook an additional 15 minutes. Serve over piping hot ravioli with freshly grated parmesan cheese.

Suggested wine: Dolcetto, Nebiolo, Gattinara

TORTELLI ALLA MUGELLANA
Potato-Stuffed Noodles in the Style of Mugello

Signora Corsi who gave me this flavorful recipe comes from the Tuscan City of Mugello at the south end of the tunnel between Florence and Bologna. When sautéeing garlic, Signora Corsi explains, you must only do so until the garlic turns *rosa*, pink or pale gold, because if you allow it to brown, *l'aglio porta l'amaro*, the garlic turns bitter. This policy on garlic is something upon which all northern regions of Italy agree. It points to one of the differences between Northern Italian and other Italian cooking where undoubtedly garlic and onions are fried "until brown."

THE SAUCE
Make a *ragù* as described on page 41 and have it piping hot at the time the *tortelli* are ready to serve. You will also need plenty of freshly grated parmesan cheese at the table.

THE STUFFING
2 medium potatoes
3 tablespoons (50 ml) chopped fresh parsley
1 garlic clove
2 tablespoons (30 ml) olive oil
Salt to taste

Boil potatoes in their jackets for 1 hour or until done; peel and mash. In mortar and pestle crush parsley and garlic. In skillet heat oil and sauté parsley and garlic briefly; do not allow to brown. Mix with potatoes and add salt.

THE DOUGH
2 cups (500 ml) flour
2 eggs
1 tablespoon (15 ml) water

On wood board place flour. Make a well and add eggs and water. Mix well and knead until shiny and smooth, about 8 minutes, adding flour as needed until dough is no longer sticky. Make a ball, cover and allow to rest 15 minutes. On lightly floured board, with light pressure of rolling pin, roll dough until very thin. With sharp knife cut dough into 2-inch (5 cm) squares. Put some of filling in center of each square. Fold one corner over the filling making a triangle and press edges tightly closed. If dough is too dry, moisten edges a bit with damp finger before folding. Holding *tortello* in your left hand, join 2 ends over your right index finger to shape into "ring." Cook *tortelli* in plenty of boiling salted water for 10 minutes or until just tender. Drain and serve immediately with *ragù*. Offer parmesan cheese.

Serves 4
Suggested wine: Lambrusco Secco or same wine served with antipasto

TORTELLONI ROMAGNOLI
Large Stuffed Noodles in the Style of Romagna

IL RIPIENO
THE STUFFING
1/2 pound (250 g) chestnuts
1 pound (500 g) ricotta cheese
2 eggs
1 egg yolk
1/4 cup (75 ml) parmesan cheese
Salt and freshly ground black pepper to taste
1/4 teaspoon (2 ml) freshly grated nutmeg

Simmer chestnuts in slightly salted water until soft, about one half hour. Drain and peel outer layer and skin as soon as cooled enough to handle. Pass through sieve. Place in bowl. Add all other ingredients, mix well and set aside.

LA SFOGLIA
THE DOUGH
6 cups (1.5 L) flour
1 1/2 teaspoons (7 ml) salt
6 eggs
2 egg whites

Place flour on wood board. Make a well and add all other ingredients. Mix well and knead, adding flour as needed until you have a pliable non-sticky dough, about 8 minutes. On floured marble or cloth-covered table, roll dough until very thin. Cut circles with rim of 3-inch (8 cm) diameter glass. Place some filling in center of each circle. Fold in half and seal edges closed by pressing them with back of a fork, thus forming the *tortelloni* with their ribbed rims. Cook in boiling salted water until just tender but still firm, about 10 minutes. Drain thoroughly and serve with melted butter and grated parmesan cheese.

Serves 6
Suggested wine: Trebbiano, Verdicchio

LASAGNE DI SIGNORA DOMASI
Baked Lasagna

The Parco delle Cascine in Florence is a lovely park, bustling with activity. Most children in the parks of Florence are immaculately dressed in what looks like their Sunday best. But regardless of attire, age or sex, as soon as a soccer ball appears they all run to the grass to be part of the game. The dexterity of their little feet in working with the ball is nothing short of astounding. No wonder *calcio* or soccer is the national game—they must be born with a ball at their feet. In this park I made one of my culinary treasure finds, Signora Adriana Domasi. She was pushing a baby carriage, taking a stroll. I came over to take a peek at the occupant, which led from oohing and ahing about her grandson to oohing and ahing about *piatti*, dishes.

LA PASTA
THE NOODLES
1 pound (450 g) lasagne
6 quarts (6 L) salted water
1 tablespoon (15 ml) corn oil

IL RAGÙ
THE MEAT SAUCE
1/4 cup (50 ml) olive oil
1 medium onion, finely chopped
3 mild italian sausages, cut in small pieces
1/2 pound (250 g) lean ground beef
2 parsley sprigs, chopped
1 celery stalk, finely chopped
1 carrot, finely chopped
1 garlic clove, crushed
Salt and freshly ground black pepper to taste
28-ounce (790 g) can italian tomatoes, or 4 cups (1 L) quartered peeled fresh tomatoes
1/4 cup (50 ml) red wine

LA BESCIAMELLA
THE WHITE SAUCE
4 tablespoons (60 ml) butter
4 tablespoons (60 ml) flour
2 cups (500 ml) milk
1/4 teaspoon (2 ml) salt
1 pinch freshly ground white pepper
1/4 teaspoon (2 ml) freshly grated nutmeg
1 cup (250 ml) freshly grated parmesan cheese

Cook lasagne in boiling salted water with oil (this, Signora Domasi says, will prevent sticky noodles). Do not overcook lasagne; they should be *al dente*, or still firm. Drain and lay on clean cloth to dry thoroughly.

Meanwhile, prepare the *ragù*, or meat sauce. In deep skillet or casserole put olive oil, onion, sausage pieces, ground beef, parsley, celery, carrot, garlic, salt and pepper. Sauté until beef is no longer pink. Pass tomatoes through a sieve and add to beef with wine. Simmer for 45 minutes.

While meat sauce is cooking make the white sauce: in saucepan over low fire, melt butter. Add flour, mixing well. Add milk all at once whisking rapidly with wire whisk until smooth. Add salt, pepper and nutmeg, continuing to stir until thickened. It should be creamy and without lumps. Remove from heat. If you must store the white sauce, dot with butter to prevent hardening of surface film and refrigerate.

In 9x13x2 inch (23x33x5 cm) baking pan, place layer of half the meat sauce, then layer of half the white sauce, half lasagne. Sprinkle with half parmesan cheese. Repeat layers of meat sauce, white sauce, lasagne and cheese. Bake in preheated 350°F (180°C) oven for 30 minutes. Remove from oven and allow to rest 5 minutes before cutting into serving size portions. A good lasagne should be neither dry nor watery but creamy and rich.

Serves 6
Suggested wine: Valpolicella, Bardolino, Grignolino

Chiostro Verde, or green cloister, of Santa Maria Novella in Florence, built by the Dominican order during the thirteenth and fourteenth centuries. While we were there, an elderly priest was briskly walking around and around the courtyard. Can you imagine a better place to do your morning jogging?

LASAGNE DI DIANA
Baked Lasagne Without
White Sauce

1 garlic clove, crushed
1 onion, finely chopped
2 tablespoons (30 ml) olive oil
1 pound (500 g) lean ground
  beef
1/4 pound (125 g) hot italian
  sausage, cut in pieces
2 teaspoons (10 ml) salt
1/2 teaspoon (2 ml) freshly grated
  black pepper
28-ounce (790 g) can italian
  plum-shaped tomatoes, or
  4 cups (1 L) peeled fresh
  quartered tomatoes
2 cups (500 ml) water
1 teaspoon (5 ml) chopped fresh
  oregano, or 1/2 teaspoon (2 ml)
  crushed dried oregano
1 teaspoon (5 ml) chopped fresh
  rosemary, or 1/2 teaspoon
  (2 ml) crushed dried rosemary
1/2 pound (250 g) lasagne noodles
3 quarts (3 L) water
2 teaspoons (10 ml) salt
1 pound (500 g) shredded
  mozzarella cheese

In large heavy pan sauté garlic
and onion in olive oil until soft.
Add ground beef and sausage,
stirring until brown. Mix in salt
and pepper. Crush tomatoes with
fork and add to pot with tomato
paste and water, oregano and
rosemary. Bring to boil, lower
heat and simmer 45 minutes.

Meanwhile cook lasagne in
plenty of boiling salted water until just firm. Drain and rinse in
cold water and lay on clean cloth.

To assemble lasagne use baking pan approximately 8x12x2
inches (20x30x5 cm). Pour thin
layer of sauce on bottom of pan.
Over it lay half lasagne. Cover
with half remaining sauce, then
half the cheese. Repeat layers
lasagne, sauce and cheese. Bake
in preheated 350°F (180°C) oven
for 30 minutes. Let rest for 10
minutes or so before cutting into
squares, otherwise it will fall
apart.

Serves 8
*Suggested wine: Pinot Bianco or
  Grigio*

TAGLIATELLE DI
UOVA ALLA NONNA
Grandma's Egg Noodles

8 cups (2 L) flour
2 teaspoons (10 ml) salt
1 1/2 cups (350 ml) warm water
7 egg yolks
2 eggs
2 tablespoons (30 ml) corn oil

Put flour mixed with salt on
wooden board. Make well in
center where you will put other
ingredients. Work together and
knead 8 minutes until dough is
smooth and shiny, using additional flour as needed to prevent
sticking. Divide dough into 4
equal parts. Working with one
part at a time form into a ball.
With palm of hand flatten ball
on a large, lightly floured marble
or cloth covered table to about 1
foot (30 cm) diameter. Using
large rolling pin, roll out dough
until very thin. This takes some
time as the eggs tend to contract
dough as you flatten it. But
eventually you will have a circle
about 1 yard (1 meter) in
diameter. Dust entire surface
with flour. Beginning at one side
of circle, make a 3 inch (8 cm)
fold. Repeat until entire piece of
dough has been folded into a flat
roll. With sharp knife, cut across
roll into narrow slices but no
more than one finger width.
Allow to dry thoroughly. Store in
a cool place in sealed containers
for future use with broth or with
sauce.

*Serves 10 with sauce, 20 with
  broth*
*Suggested wine: according to the
  sauce or same wine served with
  the antipasto*

GREMIGNA DI LORENA
Bolognese Macaroni with Sausage

1 pound (450 g) mild italian
  sausage
1 tablespoon (15 ml) butter
1 garlic clove, crushed
1 cup (250 ml) tomato sauce, see
  page 62
4 fresh sweet basil leaves,
  chopped, or $1/4$ teaspoon
  (2 ml) dried basil
4 cups (1 L) macaroni
1 cup (250 ml) half-and-half
  cream

Cut sausages along one side to
open. In large heavy pot sauté
sausages in butter. When browned add garlic and continue to
sauté until garlic is just pale
gold. Add tomato sauce and
basil. Cook until sauce is amalgamated and oily. Meanwhile cook
macaroni in boiling salted water
until *al dente* or still firm, about
10 minutes. Drain macaroni and
add to sauce with half-and-half.
Stir a couple of minutes and
serve immediately.

Serves 4
Suggested wine: Valpolicella,
  Lambrusco Dry, Cabernet

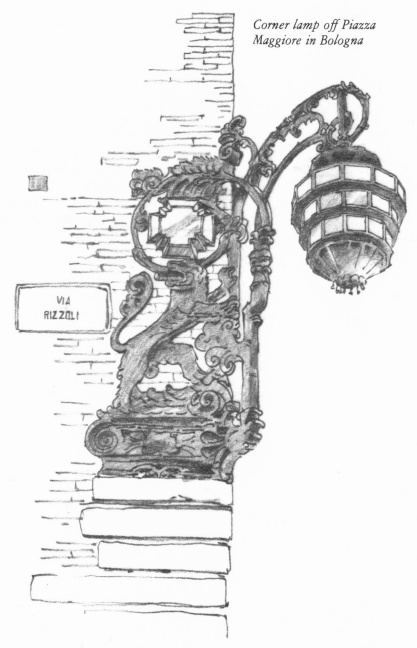

*Corner lamp off Piazza
Maggiore in Bologna*

VIA
RIZZOLI

There is a controversy regarding this statue in the Boboli Gardens, just inside the Bacchus Gate to the left of the Pitti Palace in Florence. Tourist books refer to it as "Little Bacchus Fountain" representing Pietro detto Barbino, one of the court dwarfs of Cosimo I.

My friend Paul Meserve did some fancy library research and found pictures of two dwarfs from the court of Cosimo I. Pietro Barbino being a delicate, intellectual type fellow, bore no resemblance to the generous figure on the turtle. Another by the name of Morgante was something else again, and could not be any one else but the one in the fountain. On one fact everyone agrees, and that is that the sculptor of the fountain was Valerio Cioli (1529-1599) who did many dwarf and satyr statues, and who was a pupil and collaborator of Giambologna.

BUCATINI CON TONNO ALLA MARIO
Spaghetti with Tuna

Bucatini are hollow spaghetti, and the idea is that the sauce will get into them. So says the owner of Mario's Restaurant in Florence.

1/4 cup (60 ml) olive oil
2 garlic cloves, crushed
2 tablespoons (30 ml) chopped fresh parsley
7-ounce (198 g) can tuna fish
1/3 cup (75 ml) sliced black olives
1/3 cup (75 ml) chopped green olives
2 anchovy fillets, crushed
1 small tomato, peeled and chopped
3 fresh basil leaves, crushed, or 1/4 teaspoon (2 ml) dried basil
Salt and freshly ground black pepper to taste
1/2 dried red chili pepper, crushed
1 pound (450 g) *bucatini*
Freshly grated parmesan cheese

In skillet heat olive oil. Add garlic and parsley and sauté until blond, not brown. Add tuna, olives and anchovies. After 5 minutes add tomato, basil, salt, pepper and chili pepper. Cook 20 minutes more. Ten minutes before serving cook *bucatini* in plenty of boiling salted water until *al dente* or just firm. Drain *bucatini*, and place in heated serving platter. Pour sauce over. Offer plenty of grated parmesan cheese.

Serves 4
Suggested wine: Verdicchio, Soave, or wine served with antipasto.

SPAGHETTI SCOGLIERA
Spaghetti from the Reefs

This recipe comes from Maria de Angeles, proprietress of the Villa Miramare on the island of Elba. It is made with *roba di mare,* stuff of the sea, or *frutti di mare,* fruits of the sea. When fishermen pull in their nets and remove the marketable fish, there remain all sorts of "stuff" like sea snails and shrimp. These are added to sauces for *risotto* and spaghetti. Therefore dishes *alla scogliera* are never the same, but vary according to the day's catch. I am giving you a quick and easy version of this recipe using canned clams or other canned shellfish. Of course you can use fresh shellfish when available.

1/4 cup (60 ml) parsley sprigs
1 garlic clove
1/4 teaspoon (1 ml) crushed dried hot pepper
Salt and freshly ground black pepper to taste
1/3 cup (75 ml) olive oil
1 10-ounce (284 g) can clams or other shellfish
1 pound (450 g) spaghetti

With mortar and pestle or electric blender, mash parsley, garlic, hot pepper, salt, pepper and olive oil until smooth. If using fresh stuff from the sea brush under cold running water until clean. Place clams and mussels in boiling water until shells open. Those that do not open should be discarded. If using snails place in boiling water for 5 minutes. In pot, heat sauce and sea stuff. Cook spaghetti in boiling salted water until just *al dente,* or firm, about 10 minutes. Drain and mix with sauce. Serve in heated plates.

Serves 4
Suggested wine: Orvieto, Pomino, Pinot Bianco, Corvo Bianco or wine served with antipasto

SPAGHETTI CON LE OLIVE DI GUVI
Spaghetti with Olive Sauce

Sometimes when eating at Mario's Restaurant in Florence, Mario would come, apron and all, to our table to get praises for his creation of the evening and talk shop. Guvi, a customer who was eavesdropping on one of our conversations, had to come over to get into the thick of it. This little gem is his contribution.

1 pound (500 g) spaghetti
1/4 pound (125 g) butter
1 tablespoon (15 ml) olive oil
4 parsley sprigs, chopped
4 fresh sweet basil leaves, chopped, or 1/4 teaspoon (2 ml) dried basil
1 garlic clove, crushed
20 pitted black olives, chopped
Salt to taste

Put spaghetti in rapidly boiling, salted water. Cook until *al dente,* or still firm. Meanwhile, heat butter and oil in pan and sauté all other ingredients until garlic is blond, not brown. Drain spaghetti; pour into pan, tossing with sautéd ingredients. Serve

without parmesan, for a change, or go ahead if you must.

Serves 4
Suggested wine: Orvieto, Verdicchio, Corvo Bianco or wine served with antipasto

SPAGHETTI ALLA CARBONERA
Spaghetti with Shellfish Sauce

This recipe comes from the Antica Carbonera restaurant in Venice. This restaurant is near the Pescheria, the outdoor fishmarket where amidst the hum and bustle of activity you can choose and pick from the incredible bounty of the Adriatic Sea. If you look between the columns of the Pescheria, with their capitals ornamented with fantastic sea forms, you can catch a glimpse of the glistening white Ca'd'Oro, the House of Gold, that most delicate example of Venetian Gothic along the Grand Canal.

LA SALSA CARBONERA
THE SAUCE
1 1/4 pounds (550 g) clams in shells
1/4 pound (125 g) shrimp or crayfish
1/4 pound (125 g) prawns
4 tablespoons (60 ml) cold-pressed sesame oil or corn oil
1 large garlic clove, crushed

9-ounce (250 g) can mussels
1/2 cup (125 ml) dry white wine
Salt and freshly ground black pepper to taste
1 cup (250 ml) tomato sauce, page 62, (only if making *spaghetti alla carbonera,* not risotto
1 pound (450 g) spaghetti

Brush clams under cold running water. Wash and remove shells from other fresh shellfish. Devein shrimp and prawns by making a light incision with point of sharp knife along backs and pulling out the dark vein. In high-sided skillet put oil and garlic. Sauté until garlic is blond, not brown. Add fresh shellfish, mussels with their liquid, wine, salt and pepper. Cook until clams are open, about 5 minutes. Any clams that do not open should be discarded. You can store sauce in refrigerator if it is to be eaten later in the day. When ready to serve, add tomato sauce and bring to a boil. In the meantime cook spaghetti in boiling salted water until just firm or *al dente.* Drain and serve in heated platter mixed with the sauce.

Serves 4
Suggested wine: Tocai, Pinot Bianco

Amore Umano, allegory of human love, a fifteenth century Lombardic stonework in San Marco, Venice

SPAGHETTI ALLA CARBONARA CON PANCETTA AFUMICATA
Eda Grossi's Spaghetti with Bacon

1 pound (450 g) spaghetti
3 slices (50 g) bacon, diced
4 egg yolks
1/2 pound (250 g) provolone
  cheese, shaved
1/2 cup (125 ml) freshly grated
  parmesan cheese

Cook spaghetti in plenty of boiling salted water. Meanwhile, in skillet brown bacon lightly and drain on absorbent paper. In bowl beat yolks and add cheeses. When spaghetti is done *al dente,* or still firm, drain, place on heated platter and immediately add egg mixture and bacon, stirring to melt cheese and set egg yolks. Serve *subito* (at once).

Serves 4
Suggested wine: Bardolino, Valpolicella, Corvo Rosso

VERMICELLI CON LE VONGOLE
Vermicelli Pasta with Mussels or Clams

1/4 cup (75 ml) olive oil
1 large onion, finely chopped
2 tablespoons (30 ml) tomato
  paste
1 bay leaf
1 cup (250 ml) beef broth, page
  30
10-ounce (284 g) can mussels or
  clams
Salt and freshly ground black
  pepper to taste
1 pound (450 g) vermicelli or
  very thin pasta

In saucepan heat olive oil. Add onion and sauté until it begins to brown. Add tomato paste and bay leaf and sauté 3 minutes more. Add broth, liquid from seafood can, salt and pepper. Cook until slightly thickened. Add seafood to be heated. Meanwhile cook vermicelli in boiling salted water until just *al dente,* or still firm. Drain, place in heated platter and pour sauce over. Serve at once. Some people will sprinkle with grated parmesan cheese but if you want to be authentic, you won't.

Serves 4
Suggested wine: Fiano, Greco Di Tufo, Alcamo Bianco, Verdicchio

SALSA DI POMODORO
Tomato Sauce

When recipes call for tomato sauce, you can use this recipe or canned tomato sauce.

2 pounds (1 kg) fresh pear-
  shaped tomatoes
1 small onion
1 stalk celery
1 carrot
4 tablespoons (60 ml) butter
2 ounces (50 g) prosciutto, salt
  pork or thick bacon, chopped
2 fresh sweet basil leaves, or
  1/4 teaspoon dried basil
Salt and freshly ground black
  pepper to taste

Peel tomatoes by first dipping them in boiling water to loosen skin. Finely chop onion, celery and carrot. In saucepan melt butter and sauté prosciutto and chopped vegetables until lightly browned. Chop tomatoes and add to saucepan with basil, salt and pepper. Simmer on medium heat about half an hour, stirring once in a while. Pass through a colander.

Makes about 2 cups sauce

Riso e Polenta
Rice and Cornmeal

RISOTTO
Flavored Rice Dish

The traditional Northern Italian *risotto* is prepared in an open pot adding hot broth one cup at a time allowing each to be absorbed by the rice before adding the next, but never allowing the rice to dry out. The *risotto* is done when the grains are still a bit firm and moist.

In North America we cook rice by steaming it in a covered pot. To tell an Italian that you intend to cook one of his traditional *risotti* in a covered pot will only elicit a gesture of disapproval. Therefore I give you the recipe as Italians do it. But if some day you are in a rush, and no one is looking, make sure the liquid in the pot is twice the amount of rice, bring to a boil, lower heat and cook covered for 20 minutes.

RISI E BISI
Rice with Peas

This is a typically Venetian dish, which in the days of the Doges was served during the Feast of St. Mark.

2 cups (500 ml) green peas in
   their shells
3 cups (750 ml) water
1 cup (250 ml) beef broth,
   page 30
4 tablespoons (60 ml) butter
1 tablespoon (15 ml) corn oil
1 celery stalk, finely chopped
1 tablespoon (15 ml) chopped
   onion
1 tablespoon (15 ml) chopped
   fresh parsley
1¹/₂ cups (350 ml) long-grain
   white rice
Freshly grated parmesan cheese
Chopped fresh parsley for garnish

Shell peas. Wash pea pods thoroughly in running cold water and boil them in the broth for 10 minutes. Discard pods, but save the flavored broth. In casserole put butter, oil, celery, onion and parsley. Sauté until golden. Add pod-flavored broth. Bring to boil. Add rice and cook uncovered on lowered heat, adding hot water a little at a time as needed to keep rice from drying. Gently stir occasionally. Add peas when rice is about half done and continue cooking until rice and peas are tender and moist but not mushy. Serve with grated parmesan and a sprinkling of chopped parsley.

Serves 4
Suggested wine: Orvieto,
  Frascati

Balcony in the west façade of the Palazzo Ducale in Venice, overlooking the Piazzetta. The sculptures are by Pietro da Salò and Danese Cattaneo. On the upper part you can see the Doge kneeling before the lion. Apparently there was a law at the time that stipulated that the Doge could not be portrayed any other way than kneeling before the lion of St. Mark, to prevent his misuse of power.

The Ducal Palace, built of Verona marble and Istrian limestone, typical of Venetian buildings, had all its sculptures carved especially for the building. Not so with San Marco which imported just about every ornament and piece of sculpture in it.

RISO NERO
Black Rice

This recipe comes from Antica Carbonera restaurant in Venice.

1 pound (500 g) fresh squid
1 tablespoon (15 ml) cold-pressed
    sesame oil or corn oil
1 small white onion, chopped
1 cup (250 ml) tomato sauce,
    page 62
Salt and freshly ground black
    pepper to taste
2 cups (500 ml) water
2 cups (500 ml) long-grain white
    rice

Remove and discard skin, eyes and mouth parts from squid. Discard insides, saving little shiny sac containing the ink. Rinse squid in cold water, pat dry and cut into pieces. In oil sauté onion until golden, but not brown. Add squid, tomato sauce, salt, pepper and ink that you obtain by squeezing little sac between fingers. Cook 5 minutes. Add water, bring to boil, add rice. Lower temperature and simmer covered for 20 minutes. Allow to rest 5 minutes off heat before uncovering.

Serves 4
Suggested wine: Greco di Tufo,
    Lacrima Cristi Bianco,
    Verdicchio

RISO CARBONERA
Rice with Seafood

This Venetian delight was given to me by Riccardo and Umberto at the Antica Carbonera restaurant.

Salsa carbonera, page 60
2 cups (500 ml) meat broth,
    page 30, or water
1¹/₂ cups (375 ml) long-grain
    white rice
Boiling water as needed

In casserole make the *salsa carbonera* without adding tomato sauce. Add boiling broth or water. Add rice and cook on low heat uncovered, adding more boiling water as the rice absorbs it, gently stirring with a wood spoon only as needed to prevent the rice from sticking to the bottom. The finished rice should be slightly moist, and not over-cooked.

Serves 4
Suggested wine: Tocai,
    Verdicchio, Pinot Bianco

RISOTTO ALLA MILANESE
Rice Milan Style

1 onion, finely chopped
4 tablespoons (60 ml) butter
2 mild italian sausages, sliced
2 cups (500 ml) long-grain white
    rice
Salt to taste
¹/₂ cup (125 ml) red wine
Pinch saffron
1 quart (1 L) chicken broth,
    page 32
4 tablespoons (60 ml) freshly
    grated parmesan cheese

In casserole, sauté onion with butter until translucent. Add sliced sausage cooking until slightly browned. Add rice and sauté until golden. Add wine and cook until absorbed. Stir in salt and 1 cup hot broth. Simmer until broth is absorbed. Continue adding hot broth 1 cup at a time as it is absorbed. Gently stir occasionally. With last cup of broth, add saffron. When rice is done, mix in parmesan. Cover pot, turn heat off but leave pot on burner for 5 minutes before serving.

Serves 4
Suggested wine: Franciacorta,
    Gavi, Soave or wine served
    with antipasto

RISOTTO CON FUNGHI E SALSICCIA
Rice with Mushrooms and Sausage

5 large slices dried mushrooms
1/4 cup (60 ml) water
4 tablespoons (60 ml) butter
1 small onion, finely chopped
1 mild italian sausage, sliced
2 cups (500 ml) long-grain white
    rice
1 teaspoon (5 ml) salt
1/2 cup (125 ml) red wine
3 3/4 cups (875 ml) hot water
Freshly grated parmesan cheese

Soak mushrooms in water until plump. Take them out and chop them but save the water for later. In casserole put butter, onion and sausage and sauté until golden but not browned. Add chopped drained mushrooms and continue cooking until mushrooms begin to brown. Stir in rice and salt. When rice begins to brown, add wine. When wine is absorbed add hot water mixed with mushroom water, 1 cup at a time, stirring gently occasionally and allowing each cup to be absorbed before adding the next.

When cooked, about 45 minutes, turn off heat, cover pot and let rest 5 minutes before serving. Serve with plenty of freshly grated parmesan cheese.

Serves 4
Suggested wine: Valpolicella,
  Bardolino, Grignolino,
  Cabernet

RISO CON FUNGHI ALLA MARIO
Rice with Mushrooms

2 cups (500 ml) water
1/2 teaspoon (2 ml) salt
1 cup (250 ml) long-grain white
    rice

THE SAUCE
1 garlic clove, crushed
1 parsley sprig
1 carrot
1/2 small onion
1 celery stalk
1 tablespoon (15 ml) olive oil
4 tablespoons (60 ml) butter
1 pinch dried crushed hot
    peppers (optional)
1 cup (250 ml) fresh mushrooms
1 cup (250 ml) tomato sauce,
    page 62

In casserole bring water to boil. Add salt and rice. Stir and cover. Set heat to very low and let cook 20 minutes. In the meantime prepare the sauce: Chop garlic, parsley, carrot, onion and celery *fino fino*, very fine. Sauté in skillet with oil and butter. Add hot pepper if desired. When stuff begins to turn golden add mushrooms. When mushrooms have absorbed the sauce add tomato sauce. Cook until sauce is amalgamated, about 10 minutes. When rice is done, mix gently with sauce and serve.

Serves 4
Suggested wine: Wine served
  with antipasto

RISOTTO CON BIETOLE ALLA TOSCANA
Rice with Chard Tuscan Style

1 tablespoon (15 ml) olive oil
2 tablespoons (30 ml) butter
2 tablespoons (30 ml) finely
    chopped fresh parsley
1/2 garlic clove, crushed
1/2 pound (250 g) swiss chard

Salt and freshly ground black
   pepper to taste
1/2 cup (125 ml) tomato sauce,
   page 62
2 cups (500 ml) long-grain white
   rice
1 quart (1 L) chicken or beef
   broth, pages 32 and 30
3 tablespoons (45 ml) butter
1/4 cup (75 ml) freshly grated
   parmesan cheese

In casserole put oil, butter,
parsley and garlic and sauté until
pale gold, not brown. Cut chard
into strips and add to pot with
salt and pepper. Sauté a few
minutes more. Add tomato sauce
and simmer about 1 hour. Add
rice and 1 cup broth or water.
Cook, adding boiling liquid as it
is absorbed, 1/2 cup at a time
and gently stirring occasionally
until rice is cooked but not
mushy. Turn heat off, add butter
and parmesan and serve.

Serves 4
Suggested wine: Chianti, or wine
   served with antipasto

*Campanile or bell tower of Santa
Croce in Florence*

POLENTA
Cooked Cornmeal

Polenta is the meal left after the oil, for commercial uses, is squeezed out of the corn kernels. It is coarser than the usual cornmeal. In the old days, *polenta* was considered food for the poor. Today it is enjoyed throughout Italy in different dishes.

Gina, my Bergamese friend, told me to be sure and use rock salt because refining takes away the flavor of the salt. A *bastone di legno,* or wood stick, is traditionally used for stirring the *polenta,* and you must stir only in one direction to get a smooth result.

Leftover *polenta* is served sliced and grilled with butter. Slices are dipped in flour, then beaten egg, then dried bread crumbs mixed with grated parmesan cheese and fried in butter. In Veneto they make *polenta e oselèti scapài,* page 70, and Venice is known for its *polenta pasticciata,* page 70.

Adam and Eve and the tree of good and evil. A Lombardic sculpture of the early fifteenth century, in the corner of the Palazzo Ducale in Venice.

1 quart (1 L) water
1 teaspoon (5 ml) rock salt or
    table salt
1 1/2 cups (375 ml) cornmeal,
    preferably *polenta* type

In large, preferably copper pot bring water and salt to a boil. Using a wood stick, or handle of a wood spoon, mix in one direction only, as you pour in the cornmeal slowly. Lower heat and continue cooking and stirring for about 1 hour. The *polenta* is ready when it is smooth, thick and it separates from the walls of the pot. Turn over onto the traditional round wood board or cutting board and bring to table to slice with a wooden knife, or use in one of the other recipes.

Serves 4 to 6

POLENTA E UCCELLI
Polenta with Small Birds

It was hard for me to reconcile the most gentle and kindly personality of Gina Merisio, the Bergamese woman I met in Elba, and her ability to cook and eat larks, thrushes and other small songbirds with her *polenta*. Little birds have been considered a delicacy since Roman times, and in Italian markets they are readily available. Since squabs or cornish game hens are as small a bird as my mental reservations would allow me to cook, I used them in testing this traditional recipe. If you can't take the time to make the *polenta* the right way, stirring for an hour, you can make cornmeal mush following the package five-minute recipe, but you'll have to call the dish birds in mush or mushy birds but never *polenta e uccelli*.

GLI UCCELLI
2 squabs or rock cornish game
    hens
2 small italian sausages
1 tablespoon (15 ml) cold-pressed
    sesame oil or corn oil
4 tablespoons (60 ml) butter
1/2 teaspoon (3 ml) crushed fresh
    rosemary, or 1/4 teaspoon
    (2 ml) crushed dried
    rosemary
2 leaves fresh sage, chopped, or
    1/8 teaspoon (1 ml) crushed
    dried sage
1/2 cup (125 ml) dry white wine
Polenta, page 68

Wash birds, pat dry with towel and cut in parts. Save liver for something else. With point of knife puncture a few holes in the sausage casings. In heavy skillet heat oil and butter, add rosemary, sage, the bird parts and the sausage and sauté until brown all over. Add wine, cover pot and cook 5 minutes. Move lid so pot is partially open and allow to simmer until meat is tender and sauce is oily.

While the meat cooks, make the *polenta*. When *polenta* and meat are ready, turn over *polenta* on wood serving board, make a hollow in the center and fill with the meat and meat juices. Now, *a tavola subito*, to the table right away!

Serves 4
*Suggested wine: Barbaresco,
Sassella, Chianti*

POLENTA E OSELÈTI SCAPÀI
Cornmeal and the Birds
that Got Away

This is the dish Venetians make
when the hunters come home
emptyhanded.

Skewer pieces of veal, chicken
livers, bacon and fresh mushrooms putting leaves of fresh sage
between. Brush with melted butter and grill or broil until
browned. Serve with hot slices of
polenta that have been fried or
grilled.

*Suggested wine: Merlot,
Cabernet, Pinot Nero*

POLENTA PASTICCIATA
Cornmeal Pie

In buttered baking dish put layer
of ¹/₃-inch-thick (1 cm) slices of
yesterday's *polenta,* page 68,
cover with layer of *ragù,* page
41, then with layer of sliced
italian fontina cheese, or other
fresh cheese. Next put layer of
polenta and so on. Dot with butter on top and bake in preheated
350°F (180°C) oven for 20 minutes or until hot through and
through. Offer freshly grated parmesan cheese.

Serve with no wine

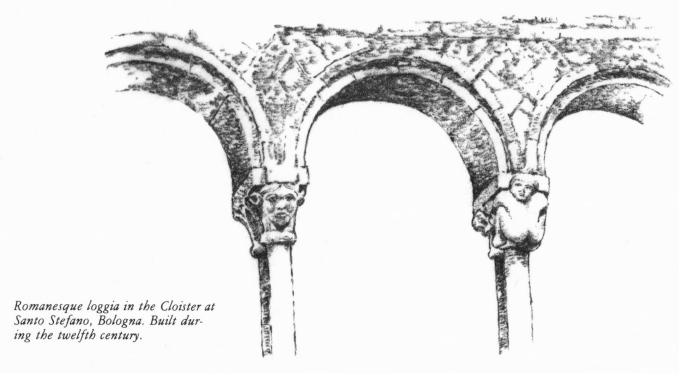

*Romanesque loggia in the Cloister at
Santo Stefano, Bologna. Built during the twelfth century.*

Uova
Eggs

Because of the continental breakfast prevalent in Italy, eggs are not served for breakfast. However, they are enjoyed for both lunch and dinner. We as Americans can continue having them for breakfast as well.

UOVA ALLA TORINESE
Turin Style Eggs

8 eggs
2 tablespoons (30 ml) butter
2 tablespoons (30 ml) chopped fresh parsley
2 fresh sage leaves, chopped, or pinch crushed dried sage

Salt and freshly ground black pepper to taste
1 pinch freshly grated nutmeg
Flour
4 tablespoons (75 ml) freshly grated parmesan cheese, mixed with
4 tablespoons (75 ml) dried bread crumbs
Corn oil for deep-frying

Put 6 eggs in pot of cold water. Bring to gentle boil and cook for 10 minutes. Cool eggs immediately in cold water. Peel carefully and cut in half lengthwise. Gently remove yolks from egg halves without damaging the whites.

Mash yolks. Set whites and yolks aside.

In small skillet sauté butter, parsley and sage briefly. Allow to cool. Add mashed yolks and mix thoroughly. Press mixture into cavities of whites. In separate bowl beat remaining 2 eggs; add salt, pepper and nutmeg. Dust each stuffed egg half with flour, dip in beaten egg and then coat with mixture of parmesan and bread crumbs. Deep-fry in hot oil until brown. Serve immediately.

Serves 4 to 6
Serve with no wine

UOVA ALLA FIORENTINA
Eggs Florentine Style

You can make this dish in individual custard cups or in prebaked tart shells made with *pasta brisée,* pie crust dough.

PASTA BRISÉE
Amounts given are enough for 4 tart shells or 1 8-inch (20 cm) pie crust. Unused dough can be wrapped in wax paper and stored in the refrigerator.

1 cup (250 ml) chilled flour
1 pinch salt
4 tablespoons (75 ml) chilled
    butter
1 tablespoon (15 ml) ice water

In chilled bowl put flour and salt. With pastry blender cut in butter until it looks like coarse meal. Add as much of the chilled water as needed to pull it together into a ball. Wrap in wax paper and refrigerate for 30 minutes to 1 hour before using.

On floured board roll dough and cut into circles. With dough circles line and slightly overlap tart molds. Trim and flute edges. Shape circles of aluminum foil into cups using a tart mold as form. Butter them on *outside* and slip into pastry lining. Fill with raw rice or dry beans and bake in preheated 450°F (230°C) oven about 5 minutes or until just barely brown. Remove rice or beans and foil and cool. Fill and bake as directed.

THE FILLING
1 pound (500 g) fresh spinach
2 tablespoons (30 ml) butter
Salt and freshly ground pepper
    to taste
3 tablespoons (45 ml) half-and-
    half cream
3 tablespoons (45 ml) freshly
    grated parmesan cheese
4 large eggs, poached
1 tablespoon (15 ml) dried bread
    crumbs

Wash spinach, shake to drain, and steam a couple of minutes in covered pan with only the water still clinging to the leaves. Squeeze thoroughly and chop. In skillet melt butter, add spinach, salt, pepper, cream and 2 tablespoons of the parmesan cheese.

Put some of hot mixture into each prebaked tart shell or buttered custard cup. Gently cover with poached egg and sprinkle with remaining parmesan combined with bread crumbs. If using tart shells, you may want to keep edges from getting too brown by protecting them with strips of aluminum foil. Bake in preheated 450°F (230°C) oven for 5 minutes.

Serves 4
Serve with no wine

*Florentine door knocker from the
private collection of Paul Boynton
Meserve*

UOVA ALLA PARMIGIANA
Eggs Parma Style

2 tablespoons (30 ml) butter
4 tablespoons (60 ml) chopped
    prosciutto or cooked ham
4 tablespoons (60 ml) freshly
    grated parmesan cheese
4 tablespoons (60 ml) chopped
    fresh parsley (optional)
Freshly ground black pepper to
    taste
4 large eggs

Take 4 individual soufflé dishes
or custard cups and generously
coat insides with butter. In bowl
mix prosciutto or ham, cheese,
parsley if used, and pepper. Press
mixture to line inside of cups,
saving some for topping. Carefully break one egg into each
cup. Sprinkle with remaining
mixture and dot with butter.

Place cups in high-sided casserole containing enough hot
water in bottom to come up to
half the height of cups. Cover
casserole and bake in preheated
450°F (230°C) oven for 10 minutes or until eggs are just firm,
not hard.

Serves 4
Serve with no wine

FRITTATA CON FUNGHI
E PISELLI
Omelette with Mushrooms
and Peas

1 cup (250 ml) shelled fresh peas
2 tablespoons (30 ml) butter
1/2 garlic clove, crushed
1 cup (250 ml) sliced fresh mush-
    rooms, about 1/4 pound
6 eggs, beaten
1 pinch salt
1 tablespoon (15 ml) chopped
    fresh parsley

Steam peas in covered pan with
small amount of water until just
tender and then drain. In small
skillet heat half the butter and
sauté garlic until just pale gold.
Add mushrooms and cook 1 minute. Put omelette pan or heavy
skillet on medium heat and melt
rest of the butter. Pour in eggs
and sprinkle with salt. Sprinkle
cooked peas, mushrooms and
parsley over eggs. Cook until
lightly browned on one side. Flip
over onto a plate, with browned
side up. Then slip omelette back
into skillet to brown other side.

Serves 4
Serve with no wine

FRITTATA CON VONGOLE
Omelette with Clams or Mussels

1 1/2 pounds (750 g) fresh clams
    or mussels
2 tablespoons (30 ml) water
6 eggs, beaten
1/2 teaspoon (2 ml) freshly
    ground black pepper
1 pinch salt
1/4 cup (60 ml) chopped fresh
    parsley
4 tablespoons (60 ml) butter
1 tablespoon (15 ml) olive oil

Scrub clams or mussels under
running cold water. Drain and
place them in large heavy skillet
with the water. Cover and place
on high heat. Shake pan as needed until all clams or mussels are
open. Discard any that are too
stubborn to open. Scoop clams
out of shells and place in bowl.
Add eggs, pepper, salt and
parsley. In an omelette pan or
heavy skillet, heat on medium
fire, butter and oil. Add egg
mixture and cook until lightly
browned on one side. Turn over
on a plate then slip it back into
skillet and brown other side.
Serve immediately.

Serves 4
Serve with no wine

Window of Baptistry in Pisa. The number of heads ornamenting this building is unbelievable. If you look carefully you will see that they come from other buildings and from different periods. They are part of the spoils brought home by the Pisan fleet.

CRESPELLE MILANESE
Rolled Pancakes Milan Style

This dish is basically crêpes stuffed with chopped flavored meat in mornay sauce which is a white sauce or *salsa besciamella* with cheese. If it sounds kind of French to you, it is not surprising. There are many dishes in France and Northern Italy which show a marked resemblance. You know the eminently French *canard à l'orange* and onion soup? Well, according to Giovanni Righi Parenti, author, poet, pharmacist, food and wine historian and a charming man, the orange duck was born in Florence as *papero alla melarancia*. The onion soup also traces its origin to Florence as *carabaccia*.

THE MORNAY SAUCE
4 tablespoons (60 ml) butter
$1/2$ cup (125 ml) flour
2 cups (500 ml) milk
1 pinch salt and freshly ground white pepper
1 pinch freshly grated nutmeg
1 egg yolk
$1/4$ cup (75 ml) half-and-half cream
1 tablespoon (15 ml) butter
2 tablespoons (30 ml) madeira wine or sherry
$1/2$ cup (125 ml) freshly grated gruyère cheese

In saucepan melt 4 tablespoons (60 ml) butter. Add flour, mix well. Add milk and quickly beat with wire whisk until smooth. Add salt, pepper and nutmeg. Cook slowly while mixing until thickened and silky. Separately mix egg yolk and cream and add to sauce. Bring to boil and remove from fire. Mix in butter, madeira and cheese. To keep surface from crusting, dot with small pieces of butter.

LE CRESPELLE
THE PANCAKES
2 eggs, beaten
1 cup (250 ml) flour
1 cup (250 ml) milk
1 pinch salt
2 tablespoons (30 ml) melted butter
Cold pressed sesame oil or corn oil for frying

In bowl mix beaten eggs and flour. Add little at a time milk, butter and salt. Blend thoroughly and refrigerate for 30 minutes.

Heat 6-inch (15 cm) crêpe pan, or other flat heavy frying pan. With paper towel dipped in oil rub inside pan. Pour in about 3 tablespoons (50 ml) batter and tilt pan in all directions to extend batter evenly. When one side is brown turn over and cook other side just until set. Rub pan with oiled towel as needed. You should end up with about 18 crêpes.

THE STUFFING
2 tablespoons (30 ml) butter
$1/2$ onion, finely chopped
1 celery stalk, finely chopped
1 tablespoon (15 ml) chopped fresh parsley
$2^{1/2}$ cups (625 ml) diced cooked chicken, beef or other meat
Salt and freshly ground black pepper to taste.

In skillet sauté butter, onion, celery and parsley until soft. Add meat, salt and pepper and sauté 5 minutes more.

PUTTING THE DISH TOGETHER
Combine one fourth of the mornay sauce with the meat stuffing and put a spoonful of the mixture on lower part of each *crespella*. Roll up and put side by side, seam side down, in a lightly buttered baking dish. Pour remaining mornay on top and bake in preheated 350°F (180°C) oven for 20 minutes or until brown.

Serves 6
Serve with no wine.

Pesci
Fish

Northern Italy is blessed with a great variety of fish and shellfish, from highly flavored fish from the Mediterranean to delicate-tasting fish from the Adriatic, besides producing abundant fish in its lakes and rivers. Fish is boiled, grilled, fried, marinated, prepared in soups and sauces, and stuffed with exquisite and varied combinations.

WINES AND FISH DISHES

White wine is considered the proper wine to serve with fish. Nevertheless, the most suitable choice of a wine depends a great deal on how the fish has been prepared. For more delicate preparations, I would suggest white wines with a light aroma and low alcohol content. Wines with more pronounced characteristics may be served with fish prepared in heavier sauces. Certain lighter red wines, such as Bardolino, Grignolino and Rossese di Dolceacqua, may accompany fish served in a very heavy sauce, but since this is rather innovative, you may produce some raised eyebrows. Experimenting beforehand might be your best bet. For treatment of wines see page 9.

One of a pair of fountains by Pietro Tacca, called the Livorno Fountains, in the coastal town of Livorno. An identical pair ornament the Piazza SS. Annunziata in Florence, where this fountain is called Fontana dell'Annunziata. According to the story, Grand Duke Ferdinand II brought them to Florence. So which are the originals is a mystery.

CACCIUCCO ALLA LIVORNESE
Fish Stew, Livorno Style

4 pounds (2 kg) assorted fish and shellfish such as eel, small lobster, squid, prawns, crayfish, shrimp, scallops, red mullet, haddock, halibut, hake
1 cup (250 ml) rock salt
$1/2$ cup (125 ml) olive oil
1 garlic clove, crushed
1 onion, finely chopped
1 carrot, finely chopped
1 celery stalk, finely chopped
1 tablespoon (15 ml) chopped fresh parsley
1 bay leaf
$1/4$ teaspoon (1 ml) dried thyme
1 cup (250 ml) dry white wine
2 cups (500 ml) tomato sauce, page 62
$1/2$ teaspoon (2 ml) crushed dried hot peppers
$1^1/2$ quarts (1.5 L) water
Salt and freshly ground black pepper to taste
16 slices toasted french or italian bread, plain or with garlic

Clean fish as necessary. Cut off heads and save them for later. Cut fish into pieces and put in flat dish over layer of rock salt for 20 minutes. (This procedure will harden fish, making it less likely to fall apart.) Clean shellfish as necessary. See page 88 if you need advice on cleaning squid.

Meanwhile, in large soup kettle heat half the olive oil. Add garlic, onion, carrot, celery, parsley, bay leaf, thyme and fish heads (remove eyes). Fry until nicely browned. Add wine and simmer 5 minutes. Add tomato sauce, hot peppers, water, salt and pepper. Cook 30 minutes. Strain contents, return clear broth to pot and keep hot.

In skillet heat remaining olive oil and fry fish until well browned. In warm soup tureen or individual warm soup bowls, place toasted bread. Cover bread with fish and gently pour strained broth on top. Serve immediately.

Serves 8
Suggested wine: Vernaccia di San Gimignano, Corvo Bianco, Trebbiano

FRITTO MISTO
Fish Fry

Fritto misto is made in most regions of Italy and it varies according to the fish locally available. Venetians prefer the use of the milder cold-pressed sesame oil instead of olive oil.

2 pounds (1 kg) assorted fish, such as shrimp, squid, sole, halibut, scallops, etc.
1/4 pound (125 g) butter
2 tablespoons (30 ml) olive oil
Flour
2 lemons, cut into wedges

Peel and devein shrimp. Remove skin, backbone, mouth parts and entrails from squid. Slice into rings; leave tentacles whole. Clean other fish as necessary and cut into pieces. Wash all and pat dry with paper towels. In skillet heat butter and oil. Dip fish in flour until thoroughly coated. Shake to remove excess flour. Fry a few pieces at a time until just brown. Drain on absorbent paper. Serve immediately with lemon wedges.

Serves 6
Suggested wine: Verdicchio, Gavi, Greco di Tufo

PESCE SPADA ALL' ACCIUGA
Swordfish with Anchovy

This dish is made not only with swordfish but other locally available fish. Salmon, fresh tuna, halibut and whiting are also suitable.

2 anchovy fillets
4 tablespoons (60 ml) butter
1/4 teaspoon (2 ml) freshly ground black pepper
4 swordfish steaks, 1/4 pound (125 g) each
1 tablespoon (15 ml) chopped fresh parsley
2 lemons, quartered

Mash anchovies, add butter and pepper. Wash fish steaks and pat them dry. Spread half the anchovy mixture on upper side of steak and grill or broil until golden, about 3 minutes. Turn over, spread with remaining mixture, sprinkle with parsley and grill another 3 minutes or until other side is golden also. Serve immediately on heated platter garnished with quartered lemons.

Serves 4
Suggested wine: Greco di Tufo, Vernaccia di San Gimignano, Corvo Bianco, Etna Bianco

One of the niches between pilasters in the Palazzo degli Uffizi in Florence. These niches contain sculptures depicting illustrious Tuscans of around the middle of the ninth century.

SOGLIOLA ALLA FIORENTINA
Sole Florentine Style

THE SPINACH
1 1/2 pounds (750 g) spinach
4 tablespoons (60 ml) butter

THE FISH
1 1/2 pounds (750 g) fillet of sole
4 tablespoons (60 ml) butter
1/2 cup (125 ml) dry white wine
Salt and freshly ground black
    pepper to taste

THE MODIFIED MORNAY SAUCE
2 cups (500 ml) milk
1/2 bay leaf
3 tablespoons (45 ml) butter
4 tablespoons (60 ml) flour
1 pinch white pepper
1 pinch nutmeg
1 egg yolk
2 tablespoons (30 ml) heavy
    cream
1 ounce (25 g) gruyère or sharp
    cheddar cheese, grated
1/4 teaspoon (2 ml) cayenne
    pepper
1 tablespoon (15 ml) freshly
    grated parmesan cheese

To make the spinach, wash and shake to drain. Cook in covered pot, without adding water, for a couple of minutes. Squeeze thoroughly and chop. Add butter while still warm. Set aside.

To make the fish, wash and carefully remove all bones. In baking dish put melted butter, fish fillets, wine, salt and pepper. Bake in preheated 400°F (210°C) oven for 10 minutes. Take fish from pan carefully and set aside. Leave remaining juice in oven until it is reduced to about 1/4 cup (50 ml). Remove and set separately aside.

To make the mornay sauce, in saucepan put milk and bay leaf over low heat until hot but do not allow to boil. Remove bay leaf. Meanwhile in small skillet melt butter, add flour and mix well. Add flour mixture to hot milk as you mix with a wire whisk. Add pepper and nutmeg and stir constantly until thickened and silky. Add egg yolk mixed with cream. Add fish juice, gruyère cheese and cayenne.

In individual shallow baking dishes or in single baking dish put a layer of spinach. Arrange fish pieces on it, cover with mornay sauce and sprinkle with parmesan. Bake in preheated 400°F (210°C) oven until golden, about 15 minutes.

Serves 4
Suggested wine: Pomino, Trebbiano, Frascati

SALSICCIA DI TONNO
Tuna Fish Sausage

This dish, if served with hard-boiled eggs, a salad and french bread, makes a refreshing summer lunch.

6¹/₂-ounce (184 g) can tuna fish in oil
1 garlic clove, crushed
1 slice french or italian bread, soaked in milk and squeezed
1 tablespoon (15 ml) chopped fresh parsley
1 egg
4 tablespoons (60 ml) freshly grated parmesan cheese
Freshly ground black pepper to taste
2 tablespoons (30 ml) dried bread crumbs
1 tablespoon (15 ml) white vinegar
Mayonnaise
1 lemon, quartered

In bowl, mash fish. Add garlic, bread, parsley, egg, cheese and pepper. Mix well, adding bread crumbs as needed to help mixture hold its shape. Place mixture in the shape of a sausage about 2 inches (5 cm) in diameter and 6 inches (15 cm) long on a piece of clean gauze or cheesecloth. Roll up and tie ends of cloth with cotton string to seal in contents. Place it in a large pot with enough cold water to cover. Add vinegar and bring to a boil. Simmer for 45 minutes. Remove roll from water. Allow to cool. When almost cold, unwrap and slice. Arrange on plate with dab of mayonnaise in center of each slice and garnish with quartered lemon.

Serves 4
Serve with no wine

Fish   81

One of the many winding streets of Assisi. Tavola calda, *literally hot table, is a modern Italian invention. It denotes places where you find diverse and tasty dishes to either eat there or take home. Usually* tavola calda *establishments are small and likely as not you will have to eat standing up.*

TROTA RIPIENA
Stuffed Trout

This dish comes from the region of Umbria, where even though there is no coastline, there are rivers that produce a most delectable trout.

4 small trout, about 1/2 pound (250 ml) each
1/4 cup (60 ml) dried french or italian bread crumbs
1 egg, beaten
1/4 cup (60 ml) freshly grated parmesan cheese
1 tablespoon (15 ml) chopped fresh parsley
1 pinch dried thyme
1/4 teaspoon (2 ml) freshly grated lemon rind
4 tablespoons (60 ml) butter, melted with
1 tablespoon (15 ml) olive oil
Chopped fresh parsley for garnish
2 lemons, quartered

Scale and wash trout; remove eyes. With sharp pointed knife remove backbone and all other bones you can manage, up to about 1 inch (3 cm) from the tail.

In bowl mix bread crumbs, egg, cheese, parsley, thyme and lemon rind. Open trout and stuff with mixture. Sew closed with white cotton thread from tail toward head. When you get to the head pass needle under the chin and through the mouth so that you sew the chin down to the body. This trick will make the fish look ferocious, but it will keep the stuffing in. Arrange trout in buttered baking pan. Brush with melted butter and oil. Cover pan and bake in pre-heated 400°F (210°C) oven for 30 minutes, basting occasionally with the pan juices.

Bring to the table in the baking pan surrounded with cooked young potatoes or cooked peas and sprinkled with freshly chopped parsley. Accompany with lemon quarters.

Serves 4
Suggested wine: Verdicchio, Soave, Corvo Bianco

SALMONE RIPIENO
Stuffed Salmon

When you have a large dinner party and you feel generous you may want to purchase a whole salmon, debone it carefully and stuff the whole fish. You'll make an impression.

1 thick piece salmon, about 2 pounds (1 kg)
1/4 pound (125 g) butter
1 onion, chopped
2 celery stalks, chopped
1 cup (250 ml) sliced fresh mushrooms, about 1/4 pound
1/2 cup (125 ml) chopped fresh parsley
Salt and freshly ground black pepper to taste
2 slices french or italian bread soaked in 1/4 cup (75 ml) milk
1/2 cup (125 ml) half-and-half cream or milk
Butter
2 lemon slices
2 lemons, quartered

Remove scales and carefully with sharp pointed knife remove backbone from salmon. Wash, pat dry, open it flat like a book and set aside.

In skillet melt butter. Add onion and celery and sauté until lightly browned. Add mushrooms, parsley, salt and pepper and sauté another minute. Remove from heat. Add bread that has been soaked in milk. Mix well. Place salmon in buttered baking dish. Put stuffing over one half of open salmon and fold other half to cover stuffing. Pour cream over. Dot with butter and arrange 2 slices lemon over. Bake, uncovered, in preheated 375°F (190°C) oven for 25 minutes, basting with pan juices. Serve immediately with quartered lemons.

Serves 4
Suggested wine: Fiano, Vernaccia di San Gimignano, Lacrima Cristi Bianco

MERLUZZO ALLA LIVORNESE
Fresh Cod Livorno Style

1 potato
1 pound (500 g) fresh cod fillets
1 1/2 tablespoons (25 ml) cold-
   pressed sesame oil or corn oil
2 tablespoons (30 ml) olive oil
1 garlic clove, crushed
2 tablespoons (30 ml) chopped
   fresh parsley
Salt and freshly ground black
   pepper to taste
From 1 pinch to 1/4 teaspoon
   (2 ml) crushed dried hot
   peppers
1 cup (250 ml) tomato sauce,
   page 62

Boil potato; peel, slice and set aside. In heavy skillet, sauté both sides of cod in sesame or corn oil until brown and set aside. Discard sesame or corn oil. In skillet heat olive oil. Add garlic and parsley and sauté until garlic is just pale gold, not brown. Stir in salt, peppers and tomato sauce. After 5 minutes, add fish. In another 5 minutes, add sliced cooked potato. When sauce is amalgamated and oily, not watery, it is done. Serve with crusty french or italian bread.

Serves 4
*Suggested wine: Pomino, Treb-
   biano, Orvieto*

BACCALÀ ALLA LIVORNESE
Dried Cod Livorno Style

This dish differs from *merluzzo alla livornese* only in that *bac-calà*, dried salt cod, is used instead of the fresh. Soak the *bac-calà* in fresh water for one or two days changing the water a couple of times to remove some of the saltiness. Pat dry, cut in 2-inch (5 cm) square pieces and proceed as with the *merluzzo alla livornese*, omitting the salt.

Serves 4
*Suggested wine: Pinot Bianco,
   Pomino, Orvieto*

SCAMPI AI FERRI
Grilled Prawns

16 to 20 fresh prawns, about 8
   ounces (250 g)
1/4 cup (60 ml) olive oil
1/4 teaspoon (2 ml) grated lemon
   rind
Juice of 1 lemon
1 garlic clove, sliced
2 parsley sprigs, crushed
Salt and freshly ground black
   pepper to taste
1 lemon, quartered

Shell prawns leaving the tails on, or you may leave shells on. Devein by pulling dark vein from head side. In bowl mix all other ingredients, except lemon quarters, and put prawns in to marinate for 3 hours covered in refrigerator. Put 4 or 5 prawns on each of 4 skewers. Grill over coals, or broil 6 inches (15 cm) from fire for 3 to 5 minutes turning once and basting with remaining marinade. Serve with quartered lemon.

Serves 4
*Suggested wine: Greco di Tufo,
   Soave, Verdicchio, Corvo
   Bianco*

A sculptured capital of a column in the lower arcade of the Ducal Palace in Venice. It depicts women inhabiting the "earthly city" in contrast to the "heavenly city" of saints portrayed in the upper gallery.

SCAMPI ALLA CARBONERA
Prawns from the Antica Carbonera Restaurant in Venice

$^1/_2$ pound (250 g) large prawns
1 tablespoon (15 ml) corn oil
1 garlic clove
2 tablespoons (30 ml) butter
9-ounce (250 g) can clams
$^1/_4$ cup (60 ml) dry white wine
8 capers
1 beef bouillon cube dissolved in
   1 cup (250 ml) hot water
1 pinch dried oregano
1 pinch freshly ground black
   pepper

Wash and remove shells, except tails, from prawns. Devein by making light incision with point of sharp knife along backs and pulling out the dark vein. In high-sided skillet put corn oil and garlic and sauté until garlic is pale gold, not brown. Discard garlic. Add butter and allow to melt. Add prawns and sauté for one minute. Add clams with their juice and rest of ingredients. Cook briefly so prawns will not get hardened by overcooking.

Serve with boiled small potatoes, or mashed potatoes, and a sprig of fresh parsley.

Serves 4
Suggested wine: Tocai, Pinot Bianco, Verduzzo

GAMBERI AI FERRI
Grilled Crayfish

In a *genovese* restaurant, high in the hills overlooking the harbor, we were served the *gamberi* as antipasto. We talked Italian to a most entertaining parrot that would nibble if we got too close. The occasion was also memorable because a raucous wedding meal was happily proceeding. As a result of the view, the parrot, the wedding and the *gamberi,* we ourselves had a joyful lunch.

20 small fresh crayfish
$^1/_4$ cup (75 ml) olive oil
Salt to taste
2 lemons, quartered

The *genovese* leave on the shell, tail and legs, so you might as well do it that way. Discard head. Wash crayfish well in cold running water. Dry thoroughly and put 5 to each skewer. Brush generously with olive oil and sprinkle with salt. Grill over coals or broil 6 inches (15 cm) away from fire, until crisp. Serve with quartered lemons.

Serves 4
Suggested wine: Greco di Tufo, Soave, Verdicchio, Corvo Bianco

Detail in the facade of the Cattedrale di San Lorenzo in Genova. When I showed this sketch to my dear friend and Italophile Paul Meserve, I said, "Look at those columns, Paul, how they turn in all uneven patterns." To which he replied with typical Meserve humor, "They did the best they could."

CALAMARI RIPIENI DI CALAMARETTI
Squid Stuffed with Little Squids

This recipe, which comes from Porto Garibaldi on the Adriatic, makes tender morsels out of the common *calamari,* squid.

THE STUFFED SQUID
2 pounds (1 kg) squid, 12 large and about 8 small
2 tablespoons (30 ml) butter
1 teaspoon (5 ml) olive oil
1 garlic clove, crushed
Freshly ground black pepper to taste
1 pinch salt
1 cup (250 ml) cooked white rice
1/4 cup (60 ml) freshly grated parmesan cheese
1 tablespoon (15 ml) chopped fresh parsley

THE SAUCE
1/4 cup (60 ml) olive oil
1 carrot, coarsely grated
1 onion, chopped
1 cup (250 ml) tomato sauce, page 62
1/2 cup (125 ml) water
1/8 teaspoon (1 ml) crushed dried hot pepper

Taking care not to tear body sack, remove from squid the film-like skin, insides, part of head above tentacles and mouth part that comes out when you press top of tentacles together. Wash inside and out and pat dry. With kitchen scissors or sharp knife chop 8 smallest squid and tentacles of 4 of the large ones. In skillet put butter and oil. Add crushed garlic and sauté until pale gold, not brown. Add chopped squid only, salt and pepper. Toss briefly and remove from fire. Add rice, parmesan and parsley. Stuff large squid with this mixture and sew open end with white cotton thread.

In heavy skillet make sauce by sautéeing carrot and onion in olive oil until tender, but not brown. Add tomato sauce and salt and pepper. After 5 minutes, add stuffed squid, water and hot pepper. Reduce heat and simmer 20 to 30 minutes. Sauce should be well amalgamated and oily, not watery.

Serves 4
Suggested wine: San Severo, Locorotondo, Fiano, Vernaccia di San Gimignano, Orvieto

CALAMARI FRITTI
Fried Squid

While on the beautiful island of Elba, off the coast of Tuscany, it was fun to wake up at the crack of dawn and wait on the beach for the local fishing boats' return. We always waited in anticipation the opening of the nets, to see what *frutti di mare,* or fruits of the sea, the fishermen had brought for us that day. If *calamari* were in the catch, signora Maria would add them to her *spaghetti scogliera,* page 59, or if they were plentiful, she would make tender *calamari fritti.*

1 pound (500 g) fresh squid
Flour
1 egg
2 tablespoons milk
Corn oil for deep frying
Salt
1 quartered lemon

Clean squid, see page 88. Wash well and dry thoroughly. With kitchen scissors or sharp knife, cut the sacklike body into rings. Leave tentacles whole; they are the treat. Heat up plenty of oil in deep fryer or heavy skillet until very hot. Beat egg with milk. Just before frying dip *calamari* in flour then in beaten egg and milk mixture. Fry in the hot oil, turning quickly. Cook very briefly because if you overcook squid it gets tough and rubbery. Serve immediately with quartered lemon.

Serves 4
Suggested wine: Elba Bianco,
Corvo Bianco, Est! Est! Est!,
Castel del Monte Bianco,
Verdicchio

Detail of a portal along a canal in Venice

One of the sculptured capitals of the lower arcade in the Ducal Palace in Venice. The lower arcade represents the "earthly city," while the upper gallery symbolizes the "heavenly city." The heads in this particular capital may be sculptures of artisans inhabiting the "earthly city."

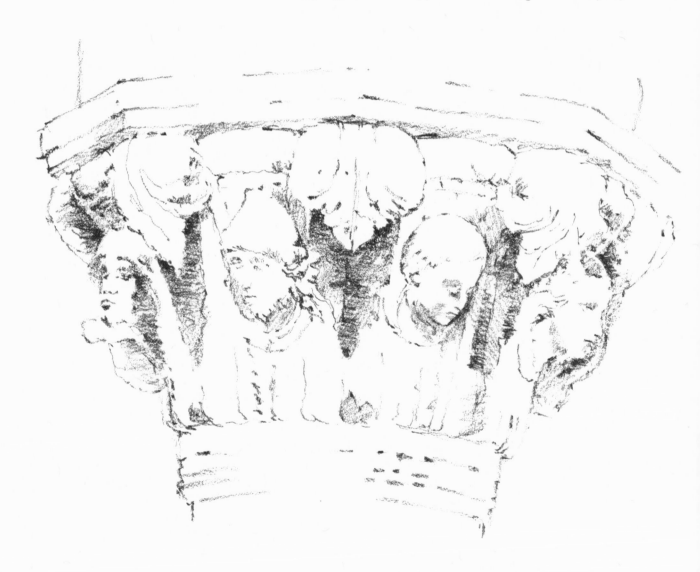

PEÒCI AL PANGRATTATO
Baked Mussels with Bread Crumbs

If you can't get fresh mussels you can use canned mussels, but you'll have to use the clam or oyster shells from your seashell collection to bake them in.

2 dozen fresh mussels in their shells, or 9-ounce (250 g) can mussels
1/4 cup (60 ml) water, mixed with
1/4 cup (60 ml) dry white wine
1/2 cup (125 ml) fresh chopped parsley
1 large garlic clove, crushed
3 tablespoons (45 ml) olive oil
6 tablespoons (90 ml) dried bread crumbs
3 tablespoons (45 ml) dry white wine
2 lemons, quartered

Brush mussels under cold running water. To open the mussels either give them a quick cooking in a pot containing boiling mixture of half water, half wine, or put them in preheated 450°F (230°C) oven only until they open. Take them out. Discard any mussel that refuses to open. Discard the half shells that are empty and place the ones with the flesh in a flat baking dish. Mix parsley, garlic, olive oil, bread crumbs and wine. Parcel out mixture to each of the mussels. Bake in preheated 450°F (230°C) oven for 10 minutes or until browned. Serve immediately with side dish of quartered lemons.

Serves 4
Suggested wine: Orvieto, Torgiano, Verdicchio

RAGÙ DI GRANCHIO
Crab Sauce

Italians say *"prendere un granchio"* when they want to say "to make a blunder," but literally translated it means to grab a crab.

Off the island of Elba there is a small crab called *margherita* which is used in making this local *ragù*. Lorena, the shopkeeper who shared this recipe with me told me to use the crab's eggs and just about everything else, which she called *"cose brutte ma buone,"* ugly stuff, but great. If you are adventurous ask your butcher to clean the crab for you and save all the edible parts from the body. Or you may simply save some of the *butter* of the crab, that golden substance, and discard all else except the white meat, of course.

1/4 cup (60 ml) olive oil
1 onion, finely chopped
1 garlic clove, crushed
2 tablespoons (30 ml) fresh chopped parsley
1/4 teaspoon (2 ml) crushed dried hot pepper
Meat from 1 large crab
1/2 cup (125 ml) dry white wine
1 tablespoon (15 ml) tomato paste
2 cups (500 ml) tomato sauce, page 62
Salt and freshly ground black pepper to taste

Spaghetti or other pasta
Lemon juice (optional)

In casserole heat oil. Add onion, garlic and parsley. Sauté until pale gold, not brown. Add hot pepper, crab meat and wine. When wine is evaporated add tomato paste, sauce, salt and pepper. Cook until amalgamated, rich and not watery. Serve over spaghetti or other pasta. Some people enjoy a lemon squeezed over the surface.

Serves 4
Suggested wine: Verdicchio, Lacrima Cristi, Soave

Bovine head on corner of the Cattedrale in Pisa, facing the Leaning Tower. Inside this magnificent building there is a curious and exquisite group of figures supporting the pulpit, done by the sculptor Giovanni Pisano.

Carni
Meats

Northern Italians prepare meats in unusually simple and delicate ways, and when selecting meat at the butcher, they insist on the freshest and most tender cuts. Even though Northern Italians eat beef and pork prepared in varied and delicious dishes, veal certainly holds for them the number one spot in the list of favorite meats. And to be right, veal must be milk fed.

WINES AND MEATS

The choice of wines that may be served with meat is more varied than with other dishes, and it offers the opportunity of reflecting the taste of whomever is selecting the wine. Generally speaking, red wines should be served with meat, but here the choice is vast. Which type of red wine? The broad spectrum of meat dishes ranges from delicate white meats to strong-flavored red meats. As a rule of thumb, the lighter and more refined the dish, the lighter the wine that should accompany it. In some cases, with particularly delicate preparations of meat, even a white wine may be served. For rustic dishes such as fried and grilled meats, it is best to serve a full-bodied wine such as Barbera, Irpinia or Montepulciano d'Abruzzo. Other preparations, perhaps richer and more elaborate, demand more renowned wines with older vintages such as Barolo, Barbaresco, Rubesco, Chianti Classico or Taurasi. An error one should avoid is that of serving an older and costly wine with a dish that requires something simple. It will inevitably result in ruining a good wine and that would ruin anybody's day.

CARNE BOLLITA ALLA BERGAMESE
Boiled Meat and Potatoes
Bergamo Style

Gina, the Bergamese woman I met on Elba, called this a *doppio piatto* or double dish because the meat is served in the same plate as the vegetables. This procedure is unusual, for in Italy the meat is generally served separately from the vegetable or *contorno*.

1 pound (500 g) boneless beef
   roast
4 tablespoons (60 ml) butter
1 tablespoon (15 ml) cold-pressed
   sesame oil or corn oil
1 onion, chopped
1 cup (250 ml) tomato sauce
   page 62, or 2 peeled
   tomatoes passed through
   a sieve
1/2 cup (125 ml) dry white wine
2 boiled potatoes, peeled and
   quartered
Salt and freshly ground black
   pepper to taste

Place meat in large pot of enough lightly salted boiling water to cover meat; allow to come again to a boil. Remove froth from surface of water with slotted spoon. Lower heat and simmer uncovered 1 1/2 hours or until meat is tender. Take out meat, cut into thick slices and set aside. Save the broth in covered jar in refrigerator to use in other dishes. In pot put butter and oil and sauté onion until *biondo non bruno*, blond not brown. Add tomato sauce and continue cooking until amalgamated. When oil begins to separate from tomato and the tomato is red not pinkish, add wine, salt, pepper, meat slices and potatoes and cook half covered until the wine is absorbed and the meat is *in-saporita*, or flavored by the sauce.

Serves 4
Suggested wine: Dolcetto,
   Inferno, Cabernet

SALSA VERDE PER CARNE LESSATA
Green Sauce for Boiled Meat

Italians serve *carne bollita*, boiled meat, in two ways. One way is to have only one kind of meat. The other way is *bollito misto*, mixed boiling, where they serve a platter piled with chunks of beef, veal, fowl, veal or pigs feet and what have you. Each type of meat is cooked just long enough to be tender but still to retain its form. The meat is cooked until almost done, then vegetables such as onion, celery, carrot and potatoes are added and served as *contorno* or side dish. Boiled meat is served with plain or hot mustard, tomato sauce or *salsa verde*.

1/4 cup (60 ml) chopped fresh
   parsley
1 garlic clove, chopped
4 anchovy fillets
1 tablespoon (15 ml) capers
1 slice french or italian bread,
   crust removed
White wine vinegar
1 hard-boiled egg yolk, crumbled
1/4 cup (60 ml) olive oil

With mortar and pestle grind parsley, garlic and anchovies. Soak bread in vinegar, squeeze and add to the contents of the mortar with crumbled egg yolk. Mix well and cover with oil. Allow to rest a couple of hours before serving.

Serves 4
Serve with no wine

POLPETTINE AL MARSALA
Meatballs with Marsala Wine

1 pound (500 g) lean ground
    beef
2 fresh sage leaves, chopped, or
    1/4 teaspoon (2 ml) dried
    crushed sage
4 tablespoons (60 ml) butter
Salt to taste
1/4 cup (60 ml) freshly grated
    parmesan cheese
1 slice french or italian bread
2 tablespoons (30 ml) milk
Flour
1 tablespoon (15 ml) corn oil
1/2 cup (125 ml) Marsala wine

In bowl mix meat, sage, 1 tablespoon (15 ml) of the butter, salt
and cheese. Remove crust from
bread. Soak white part in milk
until soft and then squeeze,
crumble and add to meat. Make
small balls out of meat mixture.
Dust them with flour just before
sautéeing in skillet with remaining butter and oil until brown.
Do not overcook; 5 minutes is
probably enough. Add Marsala
and cook a couple of minutes
more. Serve on heated platter
and pour pan juices over.

Serves 4
Suggested wine: Corvo Rosso

Sant'Antonio di Bresa, one of the saints whose relics are contained in the cathedral. A Byzantine mosaic in one of the interior arches of the Zeno Chapel in San Marco in Venice.

Gigantic stairway lion in the Palazzo dell'Università on Via Balbi, Genova

ROSBIF ALLA GENOVESE
Roast Beef Genoa Style

3$^{1}/_{2}$ pound (1.75 kg) rolled beef
    roast
2 fresh rosemary sprigs
2 fresh sage sprigs
1 garlic clove, halved
Salt and freshly ground black
    pepper to taste
$^{1}/_{4}$ cup (60 ml) corn oil
1 tablespoon (15 ml) butter
1 cup (250 ml) dry white wine
1 medium onion, chopped
$^{1}/_{4}$ cup (60 ml) pine nuts
1 cup (250 ml) beef broth,
    page 30

Insert rosemary sprigs under
strings on one side of meat and
sage sprigs on the other side.
Rub roast with cut end of garlic
clove and sprinkle with salt and
pepper. In large casserole heat oil
and melt butter. Brown meat
well on all sides. Add two thirds
of the wine. Lower heat, add
onion and pine nuts. Cook covered until wine has been absorbed (about 15 minutes). Add
broth and cook covered until it
has been absorbed. Add rest of
the wine and cook uncovered until meat is glazed in the sauce.
Total cooking time is usually 1$^{1}/_{2}$

hours. Slice and serve on heated
platter with potatoes and
spinach.

Serves 6
Suggested wine: Rossese di Dol-
*   ceacqua, Grignolino, Dolcetto*

ROTOLO DI MANZO
Stuffed Roast Beef

This Florentine recipe with its
perfect blend of herbs can be
prepared also with veal, or turkey
or chicken breasts pounded very
thin. If you don't have fresh
herbs use half amounts of
crumbled dried herbs.

1$^{1}/_{2}$ pound (750 g) butterflied
    flank steak, approximately
    $^{1}/_{2}$ inch (1 cm) thick and
    1 foot (30 cm) long
1 garlic clove, cut in half
Freshly ground black pepper
    to taste
1 teaspoon (5 ml) chopped fresh
    rosemary
1 teaspoon (5 ml) chopped fresh
    sage
$^{1}/_{4}$ pound (125 g) prosciutto or
    thinly sliced cooked ham
2 bunches spinach
1 tablespoon (15 ml) butter
1 pinch salt
4 hard-boiled eggs
$^{1}/_{4}$ cup (60 ml) corn oil
1 cup (250 ml) white wine
1 cup (250 ml) beef broth,
    page 30

Spread butterflied steak open like
a book. Rub generously with cut
end of garlic clove. Sprinkle with
pepper, rosemary and sage.
Cover with layer of prosciutto.
Cut up spinach coarsely. In
skillet, sauté spinach in butter for
5 minutes and spread over prosciutto. Spinkle with salt. Put a
row of hard-boiled eggs across
steak close to bottom edge. Fold
bottom part over eggs and begin
to roll very tightly making sure
ends are covered by meat, to
hold stuffing in. With cotton
string, tie roll in 4 places. Heat
oil and brown meat well on all
sides. Add wine. Turn heat to
low and cook uncovered until
wine has evaporated, about 15
minutes. Add broth and cook 1
more hour. Slice rolled meat into
$^{1}/_{2}$ inch (1 cm) slices and arrange
on heated platter. You may want
to surround it with cooked young
potatoes, peas or carrots.

Serves 4 to 6
Suggested wine: Valpolicella,
*   Chianti, Cabernet, Dolcetto*

ROTOLO CON FRITTATA DI FORMAGGIO
Stuffed Roast Beef with Cheese Omelette

Follow preceding recipe for *rotolo di manzo,* but instead of spinach and hard-boiled eggs, put as the last layer, before you roll it up, the following omelette:

5 eggs
2 tablespoons (30 ml) freshly grated parmesan cheese
2 tablespoons (30 ml) butter

In bowl beat eggs lightly; mix in cheese. Melt butter in large omelette pan or heavy skillet. Pour in egg mixture and fry until underside is golden. Turn omelette onto large plate and slide it back into the pan. Brown other side.

Serves 4 to 6
Suggested wine: Dolcetto, Chianti, Freisa

STUFATO BERGAMESE
Braised Beef Bergamo Style

In the northern part of Northern Italy as exemplified by Bergamo, it is characteristic of many dishes to cook the meat twice. This must be premised on the wisdom that rewarmed leftovers taste better. In making *stufato,* the Bergamese use what they call *vino nero secco* or dry black wine which is actually a type of red wine.

2 pound (1 kg) sirloin tip roast
1 garlic clove, chopped
4 whole cloves
1/2 teaspoon (3 ml) ground cinnamon
2 tablespoons (30 ml) cold-pressed sesame oil or corn oil
2 tablespoons (30 ml) butter
Salt and freshly ground black pepper to taste
1 cup (250 ml) to 11/2 cups (350 ml) water
2 tablespoons (30 ml) tomato paste
1/2 cup (125 ml) dry red wine

With sharp point of knife make *bucchi,* holes or incisions, in the meat. In some of them stuff garlic and in others clove and cinnamon. In heavy casserole over medium hot fire, brown meat in oil and butter. Sprinkle with salt and pepper. In small saucepan mix water and tomato paste and bring to a boil. Pour mixture over meat. Cover tightly and simmer over low fire for about 1 hour, turning meat once in a while. When water is absorbed and meat is almost cooked, remove from fire and refrigerate overnight. Next day cut meat into finger-thick slices and arrange in casserole. In separate saucepan heat wine and pour over meat. Cover casserole and simmer for 1 to 11/2 hours or until meat is tender and sauce is oily, not watery. Serve on heated platter, pour sauce over and accompany with *polenta* or crusty french or italian bread.

Serves 6
Suggested wine: Chianti Classico, Vino Nobile di Montepulciano, Brunello di Montalcino, Inferno

STRACOTTO ALLA EGNI
Beef Pot Roast

3 pound (1.5 kg) beef rump
   roast
2 ounces (50 g) salt pork or thick
   bacon, cut in cubes
1 cup (250 ml) red wine
1 garlic clove, crushed
Salt and freshly ground black
   pepper to taste
2 onions, finely chopped
4 tablespoons (60 ml) butter
1 large carrot, finely chopped
1 celery stalk, finely chopped
$1/4$ cup (60 ml) flour
$1/2$ cup (125 ml) beef broth,
   page 30
Parsley sprigs

Make incisions in meat and insert into them half the pork. Roll tightly and bind with cotton string. In ceramic bowl mix wine, garlic, salt, pepper and half the onions. Put meat into wine mixture and allow to marinate 2 or 3 hours, turning a couple of times to coat with liquid. In roasting pot, melt butter and sauté remaining pork and onions until golden. Take out meat, saving marinade for later, and dry with paper towel. Dust meat with flour and brown well in roasting pot with pork and onions. Add marinade, carrot, celery and broth. Cover and cook slowly, turning meat occasionally, until tender, about 2 hours. If meat is tender and liquid is too thin, remove cover until sauce thickens. When meat is done, slice and arrange on platter, keeping warm. Pass sauce and vegetables through colander or mash in blender and strain. Reheat and pour over meat. Garnish with sprigs of parsley.

Serves 6
Suggested wine: Chianti Classico, Inferno, Nebbiolo, Gattinara

BISTECCHE ALLA FIORENTINA
Florentine Steaks in the Manner of Sostanza

Trattoria da Sostanza in Florence does not like sharing recipes, but their excellent steak is so basic it is not difficult to reproduce. To make a steak *alla sostanza* begin with a well-cured T-bone steak 1 inch (3 cm) thick. Allow 1/2 pound (250 g) per person, or 1 pound (500 g) like Sostanza's. Grill over charcoal 4 minutes. Turn over and grill another 4 minutes. One minute before it's done, sprinkle with salt and freshly ground black pepper. You can vary the time of cooking depending on whether you like it *al sangue,* rare, or *bencotto,* well done. But remember if it is *alla fiorentina* it is never overdone. Serve on a warm platter garnished with pat of butter and lemon wedges, alone or with a side dish of cooked white beans.

Suggested wine: Chianti Classico

NOCE DI VITELLO ARROSTO
Roasted Veal Steak

The *noce* is a cut equivalent to the round steak.

1 pound (500 g) boneless veal steak
1 teaspoon (5 ml) crushed fresh rosemary, or 1/2 teaspoon (2 ml) dried rosemary
1 garlic clove, crushed
1/4 teaspoon (2 ml) freshly ground black pepper
1 tablespoon (15 ml) olive oil
Salt to taste
1 carrot, cut up
1 small onion, sliced
1 cup (250 ml) beef broth, page 30
1/4 cup (60 ml) dry white wine

Wash veal and pat dry. With sharp point of knife make a few incisions in the meat and stuff them with mixture of rosemary, garlic and pepper. Brush meat with oil and sprinkle with salt. In baking casserole put meat, carrot, onion and broth. Bake uncovered in preheated 400°F (210°C) oven, turning once, until broth is absorbed. Add wine and continue cooking a few more minutes until sauce is somewhat reduced.

Serves 4
Suggested wine: Barolo, Barbaresco, Chianti Classico, Inferno

OSSOBUCO
Veal Shin Bone

Ossobuco, literally hollow bone or marrow bone, is a specialty of Lombardy. In that region it is usually served accompanied with yellow *risotto* or *alla milanese,* see page 65. In Florence *ossobuco* is traditionally served alone, to be eaten with chunks of heavy Tuscan bread, which, being salt-less, goes perfectly with this flavorful dish. The marrow from the bone is considered a delicacy, so remember to provide tiny utensils to scoop it out.

I first experienced this powerful dish in the Trattoria da Sostanza, a restaurant in Florence that's renowned for its hearty, peasant-style cooking. The seating arrangement is informal and we sat with two Italians who were strangers to each other as well as to us. The topic of conversation is invariably the food at Sostanza's. The theme is invariably that this is the way food was prepared in the old days and should be prepared always. It seems there were but four entrées, all prepared with much force: an enormous grilled steak, chicken breasts sautéed in a pound of butter, *ossobuco* and one I can't remember. Because the owners were friendly but firmly secretive, I cannot with assurance state that this recipe is the same as Sostanza's, but I have duplicated it as closely as possible.

2 pounds (1 kg) veal shinbone, cut into 2-inch (5 cm) pieces
Flour
4 tablespoons (60 ml) butter
1 teaspoon (5 ml) cold-pressed sesame oil or corn oil
3/8 cup (100 ml) dry white wine
1 celery stalk, finely chopped
1 small onion, finely chopped
1 carrot, finely chopped
1/2 pound (250 g) tomatoes, without skin or seeds

FOR THE GREMOLADA
OR SPICY SAUCE
1 garlic clove, crushed
1 anchovy fillet (only 1!), mashed
Grated rind of 1/2 lemon
3 parsley sprigs, chopped

Wash shinbones and pat dry. Dust in flour. In heavy pot melt butter with oil and sauté bones until browned all over. Add wine and cook until evaporated. Add celery, onion and carrot and sauté another 5 minutes. Add chopped tomatoes, salt and pepper. Cover and cook over low heat for about 1 1/2 hours. If meat is very tender and there is too much liquid remove lid until some is evaporated. Sauce should be rich, not watery.

Mix together ingredients for *gremolada* and add to meat just before serving. Serve *subito,* right away. Do not cook the *gremolada;* it will taste too fishy if you do.

Serves 4
Suggested wine: Barbera, Sassella

COSTOLETTE DI VITELLO ALLA MILANESE
Veal Cutlets Milan Style

4 veal cutlets
1/4 cup (60 ml) flour
1 egg, beaten
1/2 cup (125 ml) dried bread
   crumbs
1/4 pound (125 g) butter
1 teaspoon (5 ml) cold-pressed
   sesame oil or corn oil
Salt to taste
1 lemon, cut into wedges

With mallet or dull side of heavy knife blade, gently pound veal to make it tender. Make small cuts around edge of cutlets to prevent curling during cooking. Dust cutlets with flour, dip in beaten egg, coat thoroughly with bread crumbs. Let sit 5 minutes. In heavy skillet sauté cutlets in melted butter and oil until golden on both sides, turning only once, gently. Lower temperature and cook 5 minutes more until done. Sprinkle with salt and serve with lemon wedges in heated individual plates or platter.

Serves 4
Suggested wine: Sassella, Valpolicella, Barbera

SCALOPPINE AL MARSALA
(Or Is It *al Madera?*)

Trattoria Silvano on Via Pratto in Florence is inordinately expensive and the old man who runs the kitchen looks mean. But he is only trying to hide a warm sense of humor and has a master's touch handling veal.

After tasting the *scaloppine al madera,* I knew I had to include the recipe in my book. So trying to ingratiate myself with the proprietor, and noticing the walls lined with napkins inscribed with drawings and messages from customers, I presented to Silvano my own sketch of a bridge on the Arno as seen from my room at the *pensione* in which I was staying. Silvano accepted it graciously and promptly hung it, smack under the coat rack. That's the last time I saw it. Undaunted, I returned and requested the recipe for the scaloppine. Being the old man's day off, Silvano himself gave me the recipe, which he called *scaloppine al marsala.* When a few days later I checked with the cook, the recipe he gave me was *scaloppine al madera.* The subtle difference between these delicate dishes is a perfect example of what the Tuscan touch is all about. So I am including both recipes for you.

SCALOPPINE AL MARSALA
Veal Scaloppine in Marsala Wine

Italian veal or *vitello,* fed on corn, wheat and milk is lighter in color and of a mildness unequaled anywhere. Scaloppine or scallops are thin round steaks, which are usually pounded even thinner before cooking. Try to buy the youngest, whitest veal possible.

Marsala is one of Sicily's most honored wines, even though its origin is credited to an eighteenth-century Englishman by the name of John Woodhouse. For this recipe you should use the almond-flavored Marsala Speciale which is a delightful dessert wine.

1 pound (500 g) veal scaloppine
Salt and freshly ground white
   pepper to taste
Flour
4 tablespoons (60 ml) butter
1 teaspoon (5 ml) cold-pressed
   sesame oil or corn oil
1/4 cup (60 ml) Marsala wine
1 tablespoon (15 ml) water or
   broth

ROSBIF ALLA GENOVESE
Roast Beef Genoa Style

3¹/₂ pound (1.75 kg) rolled beef
  roast
2 fresh rosemary sprigs
2 fresh sage sprigs
1 garlic clove, halved
Salt and freshly ground black
  pepper to taste
¹/₄ cup (60 ml) corn oil
1 tablespoon (15 ml) butter
1 cup (250 ml) dry white wine
1 medium onion, chopped
¹/₄ cup (60 ml) pine nuts
1 cup (250 ml) beef broth,
  page 30

Insert rosemary sprigs under strings on one side of meat and sage sprigs on the other side. Rub roast with cut end of garlic clove and sprinkle with salt and pepper. In large casserole heat oil and melt butter. Brown meat well on all sides. Add two thirds of the wine. Lower heat, add onion and pine nuts. Cook covered until wine has been absorbed (about 15 minutes). Add broth and cook covered until it has been absorbed. Add rest of the wine and cook uncovered until meat is glazed in the sauce. Total cooking time is usually 1¹/₂

hours. Slice and serve on heated platter with potatoes and spinach.

Serves 6
Suggested wine: Rossese di Dolceacqua, Grignolino, Dolcetto

ROTOLO DI MANZO
Stuffed Roast Beef

This Florentine recipe with its perfect blend of herbs can be prepared also with veal, or turkey or chicken breasts pounded very thin. If you don't have fresh herbs use half amounts of crumbled dried herbs.

1¹/₂ pound (750 g) butterflied
  flank steak, approximately
  ¹/₂ inch (1 cm) thick and
  1 foot (30 cm) long
1 garlic clove, cut in half
Freshly ground black pepper
  to taste
1 teaspoon (5 ml) chopped fresh
  rosemary
1 teaspoon (5 ml) chopped fresh
  sage
¹/₄ pound (125 g) prosciutto or
  thinly sliced cooked ham
2 bunches spinach
1 tablespoon (15 ml) butter
1 pinch salt
4 hard-boiled eggs
¹/₄ cup (60 ml) corn oil
1 cup (250 ml) white wine
1 cup (250 ml) beef broth,
  page 30

Spread butterflied steak open like a book. Rub generously with cut end of garlic clove. Sprinkle with pepper, rosemary and sage. Cover with layer of prosciutto. Cut up spinach coarsely. In skillet, sauté spinach in butter for 5 minutes and spread over prosciutto. Spinkle with salt. Put a row of hard-boiled eggs across steak close to bottom edge. Fold bottom part over eggs and begin to roll very tightly making sure ends are covered by meat, to hold stuffing in. With cotton string, tie roll in 4 places. Heat oil and brown meat well on all sides. Add wine. Turn heat to low and cook uncovered until wine has evaporated, about 15 minutes. Add broth and cook 1 more hour. Slice rolled meat into ¹/₂ inch (1 cm) slices and arrange on heated platter. You may want to surround it with cooked young potatoes, peas or carrots.

Serves 4 to 6
Suggested wine: Valpolicella, Chianti, Cabernet, Dolcetto

An illustrious Tuscan of the ninth century. Niche between pilasters in the Palazzo degli Uffizi, Florence.

SCALOPPINE AL MADERA
Veal Scaloppine in Madeira Wine

1 pound (500 g) veal scaloppine
Flour
2 tablespoons (30 ml) cold-
     pressed sesame oil or corn oil
1 garlic clove, cut in half
4 tablespoons (60 ml) butter
Salt and freshly ground black
     pepper to taste
1/4 teaspoon (1 ml) crushed dried
     rosemary
1/4 cup (75 ml) madeira wine

Gently pound veal with wooden mallet to flatten. Dust with flour both sides just before cooking. Meanwhile in heavy skillet large enough so meat will not overlap, heat oil and sauté garlic until golden. Discard garlic. In flavored oil sauté veal quickly on both sides, take out and set aside. Discard remaining oil and put butter in skillet. When hot add veal, salt, pepper, rosemary and madeira. Cook one more minute, turning meat once to flavor in wine. Serve by first pouring juices on warm platter, and place veal over.

Serves 4
Suggested wine: Corvo Rosso, Etna Rosso

STUFATO BERGAMESE
Braised Beef Bergamo Style

In the northern part of Northern Italy as exemplified by Bergamo, it is characteristic of many dishes to cook the meat twice. This must be premised on the wisdom that rewarmed leftovers taste better. In making *stufato*, the Bergamese use what they call *vino nero secco* or dry black wine which is actually a type of red wine.

2 pound (1 kg) sirloin tip roast
1 garlic clove, chopped
4 whole cloves
1/2 teaspoon (3 ml) ground
     cinnamon
2 tablespoons (30 ml) cold-
     pressed sesame oil or corn oil
2 tablespoons (30 ml) butter
Salt and freshly ground black
     pepper to taste
1 cup (250 ml) to 1 1/2 cups (350
     ml) water
2 tablespoons (30 ml) tomato
     paste
1/2 cup (125 ml) dry red wine

With sharp point of knife make *bucchi*, holes or incisions, in the meat. In some of them stuff garlic and in others clove and cinnamon. In heavy casserole over medium hot fire, brown meat in oil and butter. Sprinkle with salt and pepper. In small saucepan mix water and tomato paste and bring to a boil. Pour mixture over meat. Cover tightly and simmer over low fire for about 1 hour, turning meat once in a while. When water is absorbed and meat is almost cooked, remove from fire and refrigerate overnight. Next day cut meat into finger-thick slices and arrange in casserole. In separate saucepan heat wine and pour over meat. Cover casserole and simmer for 1 to 1 1/2 hours or until meat is tender and sauce is oily, not watery. Serve on heated platter, pour sauce over and accompany with *polenta* or crusty french or italian bread.

Serves 6
Suggested wine: Chianti Classico, Vino Nobile di Montepulciano, Brunello di Montalcino, Inferno

INVOLTINI DELIZIA
Rolled Scaloppine Delight

When I asked Dino at his restaurant in Florence for the recipe for his *involtini* he refused, in a most un-Florentine way. A little fancy footwork got me the recipe from his very Florentine niece, Laura, who runs a grand *pensione* on the Arno.

$^1/_2$ pound (250 g) veal scaloppine
2 ounces (50 g) prosciutto
4 fresh sage leaves, chopped, or $^1/_4$ teaspoon (2 ml) dried sage
$^1/_4$ cup (60 ml) flour
4 tablespoons (60 ml) butter
1 teaspoon (15 ml) cold-pressed sesame oil or corn oil
Freshly ground black pepper to taste
2 tablespoons (30 ml) dry white wine

Trim fat off veal and with point of knife nick edge membranes to keep from curling. Pound veal with a mallet or stone, gently, until very thin. Cut in squares, about 8 total. Put a piece of prosciutto over each square and a bit of sage in center. Roll up and either hold together with a toothpick, which is a nuisance when frying, or tie with cotton thread or twine. Dust with flour and immediately sauté in hot butter and oil briefly on all sides.

Sprinkle with pepper, add wine and cook 1 minute more. Serve forthwith with the pan juices poured over.

Serves 4
Suggested wine: Valpolicella, Chianti, Corvo Rosso

SCALOPPINE ALLA LIVORNESE
Veal Scaloppine Livorno Style

This is one of the recipes I was able to test right in the kitchen of Mario's restaurant in Florence, under Mario's bossy directions. Mario's menu calls this dish *scaloppine alla milanese* even though, as Mario explains, it really isn't, since the *milanese* version would be made without sauce. He apparently finds it easier to explain this matter than change the menu, and certainly more fun.

$^1/_4$ cup (60 ml) olive oil
1 cup (250 ml) tomato sauce, page 62
1 garlic clove, crushed
2 sprigs parsley, chopped
Salt and freshly ground black pepper to taste
$^1/_2$ teaspoon (3 ml) chopped fresh hot pepper, or $^1/_2$ teaspoon (3 ml) crushed dried hot pepper

4 veal scaloppine, about $^3/_4$ pound (350 g) in total
2 eggs, beaten
Dried bread crumbs
2 tablespoons (30 ml) cold-pressed sesame oil or corn oil

In skillet put olive oil and *rosolare* or sauté the tomato sauce a couple of minutes. Add garlic, parsley, salt, pepper and hot pepper. Lower temperature and keep at low simmer. In the meantime, gently pound scaloppine with a wood mallet or a stone until very thin and large. Dip in beaten eggs, then in bread crumbs. Fry immediately (otherwise the crumbs get soggy) in a separate pan, with very hot sesame oil, briefly on each side. Take out meat and put into the other pan with the sauce (discard the sesame oil) and simmer about 10 minutes, turning once. Serve piping hot with sauce over.

In Florence, this dish is eaten with coarse saltless Tuscan bread. A good french or italian bread will do. I have added sliced zucchini to the sauce at the time I add the veal. The zucchini absorb the sauce and act as *contorno,* or side dish, to the meat.

Serves 4
Suggested wine: Chianti, Valpolicella

VITELLO TONNATO
Veal in Tuna Fish Sauce

This quick and tasty recipe comes from Signora Venturi Secondo on the island of Elba.

4 tablespoons (60 ml) butter
7-ounce (198 g) can tuna fish in oil
1 tablespoon (15 ml) chopped fresh parsley
1 tablespoon (15 ml) sliced black olives
1 pound (500 g) thinly sliced veal scaloppine
1 lemon, quartered

In skillet melt butter. Mix in tuna fish, parsley and olives and sauté briefly. Add veal and cook only a few minutes each side. Serve with quartered lemon and crusty french or italian bread and butter.

Serves 4
Suggested wine: Frascati, Pinot Bianco, Fiano

AGNELLO TOSCANO CON OLIVE NERE DI GAETA
Tuscan Lamb with Greek Type Olives

Italian cities abound in small coffee shops where one goes for a break in the daily affairs. There are spiked drinks, pastries, coffee, tobacco and other various and sundry items. Bar Tabacchi Ennio in Via dei Neri in Florence is run by the Magnelli, a delightful couple that typifies the generosity, effervescent liveliness and humor of the Florentines. It was at one of the little tables toward the back that Maria would sit, always willingly, with me to talk food. She gave the credentials of this recipe of hers by bestowing on it the ultimate Italian symbol of perfection, kissing the tips of all five fingers while looking at the ceiling.

1 1/4 pound (550 g) lamb stew meat
Flour
1/4 cup (60 ml) olive oil
1 garlic clove, crushed
1/2 teaspoon (3 ml) dried rosemary, or 1 teaspoon (5 ml) chopped fresh rosemary
4 tomatoes, peeled, seeded and chopped, or 16-ounce (450 g) can Italian-style tomatoes
Salt and freshly ground black pepper to taste
1/4 pound (125 g) black olives from Gaeta, or Greek-type olives, cut in half and pitted

Dust pieces of meat in flour. In casserole fry meat in olive oil until well browned. Add garlic and rosemary. When garlic is pale gold, add chopped tomatoes, salt, pepper and olives. Cover and cook over low heat 45 minutes or until meat is tender.

Serves 4
Suggested wine: Valpolicella, Merlot, Cabernet

TRIPPA ALLA FIORENTINA
Armando's Tripe Florentine Style

Ristorante Armando happens to be a few blocks away from the opera house in Florence. During the opera season, while eating supper there, we often would hear small parts of arias being sung from the tables at the back of the room. Upon a thorough and impolite scrutiny we noticed that the singers were customers and that invariably they were consuming healthy portions of *trippa alla fiorentina*. Soon we found out that the magnificent voices belonged to members of the opera. As to why *trippa*, we could only speculate it might have something to do with the concept of singing from the gut. Whatever the answer, the atmosphere was charming, the *trippa*, superb.

3 parsley sprigs
1 carrot
1 celery stalk
1 small onion
1 tablespoon (15 ml) olive oil
1 1/2 pounds (750 g) tripe
1 cup (250 ml) tomato sauce, page 62
1 cup (250 ml) water
4 potatoes, diced (optional)

Chop parsley, carrot, celery and onion *fino fino* or very fine. In heavy skillet heat oil and sauté chopped vegetables, stirring often, until tender but not browned. Cut tripe into strips 1/2 inch (1 cm) by 2 inches (5 cm). Add tripe, tomato sauce and water to vegetables and cook until tripe is tender, about 1 1/2 hours. Serve with plenty of crusty french or italian bread to sop up juice.

If you wish to make a one-dish meal, add diced potatoes and 1 more cup (250 ml) water when you add the tripe. Sing *fortissimo!*

Serves 4
Suggested wine: Chianti

TRIPPA IN SALSA VERDE
Tripe in Green Sauce

1 1/2 pounds (750 g) tripe
2 cups (500 ml) water
1 garlic clove
1/2 cup (125 ml) chopped fresh parsley
1/4 cup (75 ml) freshly grated parmesan cheese
1 hard-boiled egg yolk
3 tablespoons (45 ml) olive oil
6 capers
4 anchovy fillets
1 tablespoon (15 ml) vinegar
Salt to taste

Wash and cut tripe into half-inch-wide strips. Cut strips into pieces 2 inches long. In saucepan simmer tripe in water until tender, about 1 1/2 hours, then drain thoroughly. With mortar and pestle grind all other ingredients, or process in blender at high speed until smooth. Add sauce to tripe and cook 5 minutes more.

Serves 4
Serve with no wine

Detail of mosaic floor in San Marco in Venice. Due to the floods that convert the Piazza San Marco into a lake, these mosaic floors are constantly being repaired. Unfortunately, the damage to them seems faster than the loving hands of the Italians can restore them.

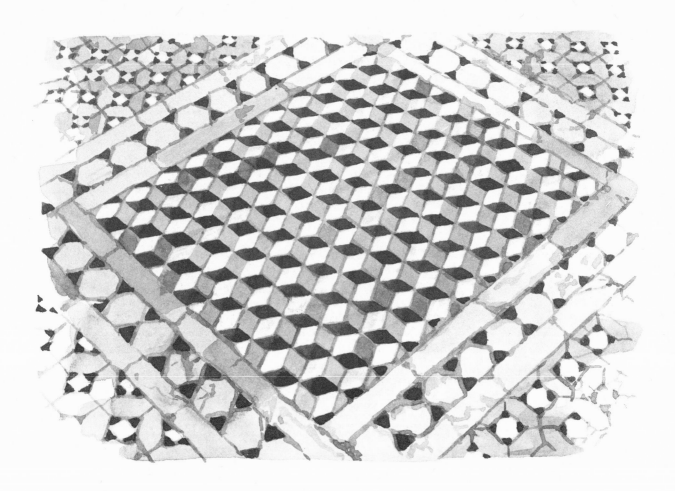

FEGATO ALLA VENEZIANA
Liver Venetian Style

LA POLENTA

Tradition calls for *polenta* to be cooked in a copper pan stirred continually with a *bastone di legno* or wood stick, and always in the same direction. And when served it is presented to the table on a round wood board.

7 cups (1.75 L) water
Salt to taste
1 pound (500 g) *polenta* or corn-meal
4 tablespoons (60 ml) butter

In large pot, heat water and salt over hot fire. When boiling add the cornmeal by pouring it, as you stir with a wood stick or spoon. In about 40 minutes, if your arm hasn't fallen off, the *polenta* will be pulling away from the pot sides and will be thick. Add butter, mix thoroughly and remove from fire. Or you can make it according to the cornmeal package recipe. But don't call it *polenta,* call it mush.

IL FEGATO

1 large onion
1/2 pound (225 g) fresh calfs' liver or beef liver
2 tablespoons (30 ml) butter
1 tablespoon (15 ml) cold-pressed sesame oil or corn oil
Salt and freshly ground black pepper to taste

Slice onion very fine. Slice liver as thin as you can possibly slice it. In skillet, heat butter and oil. Add onions and sauté until just blond, not brown. Set onions aside and keep warm. In the butter and oil remaining in pan, sauté liver quickly over brisk heat, tossing to brown both sides, no more than 3 minutes. Season with salt and pepper and serve immediately with onions and hot *polenta* slices.

Serves 4
Suggested wine: Valpolicella, Merlot, Cabernet

BRACIOLE DI MAIALE ALLA MODENESE
Pork Chops Modena Style

If you grow your own herbs substitute twice the amount of fresh for dry. The flavor is much nicer using fresh herbs, and they are easy to grow near a sunny window.

1 garlic clove
1/4 teaspoon (2 ml) dried rosemary
1/8 teaspoon (1 ml) dried thyme
1/8 teaspoon (1 ml) dried sage
1/4 teaspoon (2 ml) salt
1/4 teaspoon (2 ml) freshly ground black pepper
2 teaspoons (10 ml) olive oil
4 lean pork chops, boned
1/2 cup (125 ml) water
1/4 cup (60 ml) dry white wine

With mortar and pestle crush garlic, herbs, salt and pepper; add olive oil and grind well. Flatten pork chops lightly with wood mallet. Rub pork chops with herb mixture and allow to *insaporire,* or flavor, for 10 minutes. Place in heavy skillet, add water, and bring to boil. Cover, lower temperature to medium and simmer for 20 minutes or until water has evaporated, turning chops once or twice. Remove lid and allow chops to brown in their own fat, both sides. Add wine and continue cooking until almost completely evaporated. Rub both sides of chops in sauce at bottom of pan to coat.

Serves 4
Suggested wine: Lambrusco Secco, Sangiovese, Chianti Classico

ARISTA ALLA ARMANDO
Grilled Pork Chops

4 center-cut pork chops with
  bone
1 sprig fresh rosemary, or
  $1/2$ teaspoon (3 ml) dried rosemary, crushed
1 garlic clove, crushed
Salt and coarsely chopped black
  pepper to taste
1 lemon, cut into wedges

With sharp point of knife make
incisions into the meat and stuff
them with mixture of rosemary
and garlic. Sprinkle chops with
salt and pepper both sides. Grill
over hot coals or under broiler,
turning once or twice, until
cooked through but still juicy.
Serve with lemon wedges.

Serves 4
Suggested wine: Barolo, Chianti
  Classico, Brunello di Montal-
  cino

MAIALE E FAGIOLI BERGAMESE
Pork and Beans Bergamo Style

The town of Bergamo in the
center of Lombardy is nowhere
near the sea. So it was with surprise and amusement that while
on the island of Elba we saw a
group of strong, fully equipped
scuba divers display on their
chests an insignia reading
Bergamo Sub. We thereafter had
the opportunity to hear stories of
this active club whose members
travel along the coast of Italy and
its islands, enjoying the marine
life that is so plentiful and varied
in the warm, clear waters of the
Mediterranean.

Gina, wife of Arnaldo Merisio,
the senior diver, shared with me
this and several other tasty
bergamese recipes while keeping
an eye on effervescent Emiliana,
their five-year-old. One day I
picked some green almonds from
a tree, for Emiliana. She hadn't
known that the tender translus-
cent young nuts of the almond
were edible, but she was game.
After thoughtfully chomping on
a few she looked up at me with
huge dark eyes and said in her
high-pitched precise Italian:
*"Com'è brava in cose di man-
giare"* ("How clever you are in
things to eat").

4 slices, $1/4$ pound (125 g) each,
  lean pork meat without bone
6 bacon slices
1 pinch crushed dried sage
1 pinch crushed dried rosemary
1 tablespoon (15 ml) butter
1 tablespoon (15 ml) cold-pressed
  sesame oil or corn oil
1 tablespoon (15 ml) tomato
  paste
$1/2$ cup (125 ml) beef broth, page
  30, or water
2 cups (500 ml) cooked white
  beans
Salt to taste

With wood mallet pound pork
until flattened and extended. Fry
bacon until crisp, drain on absorbent paper and crumble. On
each slice of pork put some
crumbled bacon, sage and rosemary. Roll up and hold together
with toothpicks or tie with cotton
string. In casserole heat butter
and oil and fry the pork rolls until golden all over. Add tomato
paste dissolved in broth or water
and cook for 5 minutes. Add
beans and cover. Let simmer 15
or 20 minutes, turning meat once
or twice. Add salt and continue
cooking uncovered a few minutes
so liquid is absorbed.

Serves 4
Suggested wine: Barbera,
  Taurasi, Corvo Rosso

Window detail in the Cortile di Pilato at the Seven Churches of Santo Stefano in Bologna

Pollame
Poultry

POLLAME
Poultry

Northern Italy is renowned for its plump and succulent chickens. Breast of chicken, like veal, is highly prized and is used in numerous subtle preparations, with wines, cheeses, prosciutto and various spices.

WINES AND POULTRY

As with meat, the choice of wines which may accompany poultry is quite vast and depends a great deal on the preparation of the dish. When serving poultry, it is best to stick to young, medium-bodied red wines, or slightly aged reds. Game birds would be an exception since delicate types such as pheasant and guinea fowl require pure class wines of a light consistency, such as Dolcetto, Cabernet and Chianti. Other game birds such as duck, partridge and woodcock require older wines with greater body such as Brunello di Montalcino or Vino Nobile di Montepulciano.

PETTI DI POLLO RIPIENI
Stuffed Chicken Breasts

4 chicken breast halves, without skin or bones
Salt and freshly ground black pepper to taste
1 teaspoon (5 ml) butter
4 eggs, lightly beaten
4 slices Italian fontina cheese
4 slices prosciutto or thinly sliced ham
1 tablespoon (15 ml) corn oil
1 tablespoon (15 ml) butter
1 cup (250 ml) chicken broth

Wash breasts and pat dry with towel. With sharp knife slice breasts so you can open them flat like an open book. Pound with a wood mallet to extend them. Sprinkle with salt and pepper. In small pan melt butter and scramble eggs. Divide scrambled eggs among the chicken breasts, placing a portion upon the center of each. Cover egg with 1 slice of fontina cheese and 1 slice prosciutto or ham. Fold sides of breast over stuffing and roll up beginning at one end, making sure all filling is concealed inside the breast meat. Tie with piece of cotton string. In skillet brown rolls in oil and butter. Add broth, lower heat and cook uncovered 3/4 hour. Before serving, slice into 1/2-inch (1.5 cm) slices, removing ties.

Serves 4
Suggested wine: Valpolicella, Bardolino

POLLO AL DIAVOLO
Devil's Hot Chicken

They say that this dish acquired its name because some people prepare it with great quantities of cayenne pepper, and those who eat it, upon feeling their mouths burn up, are tempted to send to the devil both the chicken and the cook.

4 frying chicken breast halves
2 tablespoons (30 ml) melted
   butter
Salt to taste
1/2 teaspoon (2 ml) crushed dried
   hot peppers or cayenne pepper

Remove skin and bones from breasts and if you wish, save them for broth. Wash breasts and pat dry. Grill on a grate or broil 5 inches (13 cm) from the fire about 5 minutes or until meat begins to brown. Brush with butter, sprinkle with salt and hot pepper and turn over. Cook other side for 5 minutes, brush with butter, sprinkle with salt and hot pepper and continue grilling 1 more minute. Serve on heated plates.

Serves 4
Suggested wine: Chianti,
   Valpolicella, Dolcetto

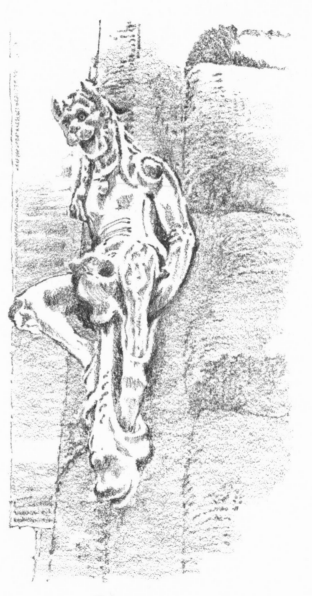

Lucifero, or Lucifer, a corner detail on a building in Florence

SPIEDINO DI POLLO
Chicken Kabobs

This recipe comes from the area around Lake Como in Lombardy. You can ask your butcher to bone the chicken for you, otherwise use a sharp knife and try to remove the muscles as whole as possible. Save the skin, bones and giblets for making broth, which you can refrigerate in covered jars for other recipes.

1 whole frying chicken, about
   3 pounds (1.5 kg)
1/4 pound (125 g) cooked ham
2 tablespoons (30 ml) chopped
   fresh parsley
1 teaspoon (5 ml) chopped fresh
   sweet basil or 1/4 teaspoon
   (2 ml) dried sweet basil
1/4 cup (60 ml) corn oil
Salt

Bone chicken and cut into thin slices; pound a little with a wood mallet to flatten them. Put small piece of ham in center. Sprinkle with parsley and basil. Roll up and thread through skewers. Brush lightly with oil. Grill over charcoal or under broiler turning frequently until lightly browned, about 10 minutes. Sprinkle very lightly with salt and serve on the skewers immediately.

Serves 4
Suggested wine: Barbera,
   Rubesco, Dolcetto

POLLO AL MODO DI SOSTANZA
Chicken Breasts in the Style of Sostanza

4 frying chicken breast halves
2 tablespoons (30 ml) cold-
   pressed sesame oil or corn oil
1 garlic clove
Flour
Salt and freshly ground black
   pepper to taste
2 tablespoons (30 ml) butter

Wash chicken breasts and pat dry with towel. With sharp knife remove bones and skin leaving meat in one piece. Save bones and skin to make broth for other dishes.

   In skillet heat oil and sauté whole garlic clove until pale gold, not brown. Discard garlic. Dust chicken breasts in flour and sauté in the garlic-flavored oil briefly on each side. Remove breasts to a plate. Discard the oil and wipe skillet with paper towel. Melt butter in skillet, sauté breasts briefly on each side and serve immediately.

Serves 4
Suggested wine: Sangiovese,
   Rosso Conero, Merlot

POLLO ALLA MARENGO
Chicken Marengo

Napoleon must have been rather pleased with his victory in the battle of Marengo to have given the name of Marengo not only to his horse but to his chicken as well. The story goes that in the confusion after the battle, the cook could not find his supplies to make supper, so using ingenuity and a stolen chicken, he improvised. Napoleon was so delighted with the concoction that he bestowed upon it the name of his successful battle.

   This version of chicken Marengo is quite different from recipes in most contemporary Italian cookbooks. It is based upon the recipe of Pellegrino Artusi, the ''grandfather'' of Italian cookbook authors.

4 frying chicken breast halves
1/2 carrot
1/2 celery stalk
2 cups (500 ml) water

2 tablespoons (30 ml) butter
1 tablespoon (15 ml) cold-pressed
    sesame oil or corn oil
Salt and freshly ground black
    pepper to taste
1/4 teaspoon (2 ml) freshly grated
    nutmeg
1 tablespoon (15 ml) flour
3/8 cup (100 ml) dry white wine
2 parsley sprigs, chopped
1/2 lemon

Wash chicken breasts and pat dry with towel. With sharp knife remove bones and skin leaving meat in one piece. In pot put bones, skin, carrot, celery and water. Bring to boil, lower heat and simmer until it has condensed to about 1 cup broth.

Strain and skim fat off top. Save clear broth until later. In skillet heat butter and oil. Add breasts and sauté briefly each side. Sprinkle with salt, pepper and nutmeg. Remove breasts onto a plate. To the butter and oil in the skillet add flour, mix well. Add wine and stir. Add broth; stir until smooth. Add breasts and simmer on low fire turning once or twice until meat is cooked and sauce is reduced to gravy consistency. Serve on heated platter sprinkled with parsley and lemon juice.

Serves 4
Suggested wine: Barbera,
    Dolcetto

POLLO AL PEPERONE
Chicken with Bell Pepper

1 frying chicken, about 2 1/2
    pounds (1.25 kg) cut up
1/4 cup (60 ml) cold-pressed
    sesame oil or corn oil
1 medium onion, chopped
1 green bell pepper, thinly sliced
Salt and freshly ground black
    pepper to taste
1 cup (250 ml) dry white wine

Wash chicken and pat dry. (Use liver in some other recipe.) In casserole brown chicken in hot oil. Add onion, bell pepper, salt and pepper. When onion is soft add wine, cover and simmer over low fire for 1 hour, or until chicken is tender, turning chicken as needed during cooking. Last few minutes remove lid to glaze meat in its juices.

Serves 4
Suggested wine: Bardolino,
    Grignolino, Freisa

Detail from bronze door in the
Cathedral in Pisa

POLLO IN UMIDO
ALLA ELIO BOSCHI
Stewed Chicken

Elio sold me a lovely Italian leather purse, but I would not leave his store in Florence before I got hold of his favorite chicken recipe.

IL POLLO
THE CHICKEN
1/4 cup (60 ml) olive oil
1 onion, chopped
1 garlic clove, crushed
1 carrot, finely chopped
1 celery stalk, finely chopped
1 frying chicken, about 3 pounds
   (1.5 kg), cut up, washed
   and dried
1 cup (250 ml) tomato sauce,
   page 62
Salt and freshly ground black
   pepper to taste
2 cups (500 ml) water
1/2 cup (125 ml) dry white wine

IL CONTORNO
THE VEGETABLE
2 cups (500 ml) cauliflower, or
   celery stalks or artichoke hearts
1/2 cup (125 ml) flour
1 egg, beaten
2 tablespoon (30 ml) butter
1 tablespoon (15 ml) olive oil

In large heavy pan sauté onion, garlic, carrot and celery in olive oil until soft but not brown. Add chicken and sauté until brown. Add tomato sauce, salt, pepper and water. Bring to boil, cover and lower heat. Cook until water is absorbed and chicken is tender, approximately 1 hour. If chicken is a tough one add more water and continue cooking until done. Add wine and cook uncovered until evaporated.

Meanwhile cut cauliflower or other vegetable into bite-sized pieces, dust them in flour, dip them in egg and immediately sauté in separate skillet with butter and olive oil until brown. Remove chicken to warm platter. Put sauteéd vegetable into pan with chicken juices to get flavored and serve them with the chicken.

Serves 4
Suggested wine: Lambrusco Secco, Sangiovese, Merlot

POLLO AL LIMONE
Chicken with Lemon

This simple and delicate dish comes from the city of Ravenna near the Adriatic Sea in the Emilia-Romagna region. Save the giblets for other dishes; you can use the liver to make *crostini di fegatini*, page 24, and the rest to make broth, page 32.

1 whole frying chicken, about 3
   pounds (1.5 kg)
Salt and freshly ground black
   pepper to taste
1 teaspoon (5 ml) chopped fresh
   sage, or 1/2 teaspoon (3 ml)
   crushed dried sage
3 lemons

Wash chicken inside and out and pat dry. Rub salt, pepper and sage all over chicken inside and out. Cut 1 lemon in 4 pieces and place inside cavity of bird; tie legs together with cotton string. Squeeze juice of other 2 lemons all over body. Roast in uncovered pan in preheated 350°F (180°C) oven, basting occasionally for 1 hour or until browned.

Serves 4
Suggested wine: Lambrusco Secco, Sangiovese

COLLO DI POLLO
ALLA CASALINGA
Home-Style Stuffed
Chicken Necks

One early morning in Florence, while trading recipes with Mario in the kitchen of his restaurant, I made for him my mother's recipe of stuffed chicken neck skins. He watched while I painstakingly sewed the ends with needle and thread. When the dish was cooked he tasted it, kissed the tips of his fingers in approval and in his polite Italian said, "Now I'll make you *my* mother's *collo di pollo.*" When he had made his version of the stuffing he took bits of string and tied the ends closed in ten seconds flat. Mario's recipe, which I will give you, comes from the region of the Marches, where Mario's mother was born.

Have your butcher select skins that are long and untorn.

4 whole chicken neck skins
4 chicken livers
4 tablespoons (60 ml) butter
1/4 cup (60 ml) finely chopped
   fresh parsley
1/2 teaspoon (3 ml) salt
1/4 teaspoon (2 ml) freshly
   ground black pepper
1 garlic clove, crushed
2 tablespoons (30 ml) olive oil
4 eggs, beaten
1 pinch crushed dried hot peppers (optional)
1 1/2 cups (350 ml) dried bread
   crumbs
2 tablespoons (30 ml) butter
1 tablespoon (15 ml) olive oil
1/2 cup (125 ml) dry white wine

Wash neck skins and dry with towel. Set aside. In skillet sauté livers in butter only until all pink

is gone. Remove from fire. Mash livers in butter with fork, add parsley, salt, pepper, garlic, oil, eggs and hot pepper, if used. Mix well. Add as much bread crumbs as you need so the stuffing will not be runny. Tie one end of each neck skin closed with a bit of cotton string. Through open end, fill skins with the stuffing and tie other end closed. In skillet sauté stuffed skins in butter and oil until brown on all sides. Add wine, cover, lower temperature and simmer for 30 minutes or until wine is absorbed. Serve hot.

Serves 4
*Suggested wine: Chianti, Chianti
   Classico*

Tower in Porto Civitanova, the Marches

POLLO ALLA BIRRA
Chicken in Beer

In this dish you use the whole chicken and even the giblets, if you wish, but not the liver. So either save the liver for some other dish or sauté it briefly in butter, sprinkle with salt and eat it on the spot. Although many people don't associate beer with Italian cooking, this recipe came from a friend in Florence.

If you want to make this dish using a stewing chicken you should use 2 cans of beer and expect it to take much longer in cooking because it is a tougher bird.

1 whole frying chicken, about 3
    pounds (1.5 kg)
1 teaspoon (5 ml) fresh
    rosemary, or 1/2 teaspoon (3
    ml) dried rosemary
1 teaspoon (5 ml) fresh sage, or
    1/2 teaspoon (3 ml) dried sage
1 teaspoon (5 ml) salt
1/4 teaspoon (2 ml) freshly
    ground black pepper
1 garlic clove
1 bottle or can of beer

Wash whole chicken inside and out and pat dry. With mortar and pestle crush rosemary, sage, salt, pepper and garlic together. Rub this mixture on entire body of bird inside and out. Set it in a casserole not much bigger than the chicken itself and add enough beer to cover bird. Bring to boil, cover, lower temperature to medium and simmer for 45 minutes. Turn chicken over and cover again. Cook until tender and beer is absorbed. If chicken is tender before beer is absorbed remove lid to allow evaporation and cook until just an oily sauce remains. Gently glaze chicken in the sauce and serve.

Serves 4
*Suggested wine: Vernaccia di San
    Gimignano, Fiano, Trebbiano*

TACCHINO CON SALSICCIA
Turkey with Sausage

This tasty recipe comes from Bergamo in Central Lombardy.

2 pounds (1 kg) turkey parts like
    legs and thighs
4 hot italian sausages
4 tablespoons (60 ml) butter
Salt and freshly ground black
    pepper to taste
1/2 cup (125 ml) dry white wine
2 cups (500 ml) chicken broth,
    page 32, or water
Mashed potatoes

Wash turkey parts and pat dry with towel. In large heavy pot brown turkey and sausages in butter. Prick sausages with fork on both sides. Add salt and pepper. When nicely browned add wine and cook until evaporated. Add broth. Bring to boil, cover pot, lower heat and cook for 1 1/2 hours or until turkey is tender. Turn occasionally during cooking. The last 15 minutes of cooking remove lid and allow meat to glaze in the thick sauce. Serve on heated platter surrounded by a ring of mashed potatoes extruded through a pastry nozzle. Pour the sauce over the meat.

Serves 4
*Suggested wine: Barbera, Taurasi,
    Cabernet*

PICCIONI ALLA GRIGLIA
Grilled Squabs

The menu at Ristorante Mario does not include *piccioni*. When I commented on that fact, Mario promised to cook them the next evening. In true Mario fashion, tomorrow happened three days later, but perseverance paid off, his *piccioni alla griglia* were superb. If you are like my son who would rather feed pigeons than eat them, you can substitute rock cornish game hens.

Many restaurants in Northern Italy grill their meats on spits placed in front of the fire instead of over it. This arrangement cooks the meat by radiant heat so it does not absorb the products of combustion. This allows the mild taste of some meats and fish not to be dominated by the taste of wood or charcoal.

2 large squabs or 4 small ones
Juice of 1 large lemon
4 fresh sage leaves, chopped, or 1/2 teaspoon (3 ml) crushed dried sage
Salt and freshly ground black pepper to taste
1 tablespoon (15 ml) corn oil
1 tablespoon (15 ml) melted butter
1 lemon, cut into wedges

With sharp knife or kitchen scissors cut along breast bone and open squabs flat. Wash and pat dry. Rub them all over with mixture of lemon juice, sage, salt and pepper. Let marinate in refrigerator for 15 to 30 minutes. Drain, brush with oil and butter, and grill both sides until done but still juicy. Brush with oil and butter during grilling. Serve with lemon wedges.

Serves 4
Suggested wine: Chianti Classico, Barbera

Some eat pigeons, some feed pigeons

ANATRA AL CHIANTI
Duck in Chianti Wine

This delightful recipe is based on Chianti, the eminent wine from the heart of Tuscany.

1 whole duck, about 4 pounds (2 kg), with giblets
1/4 cup (60 ml) olive oil
2 bay leaves
Salt and freshly ground black pepper to taste
2 cups (500 ml) Chianti wine
1 cup (250 ml) water
2 slices prosciutto or ham
1 tablespoon (15 ml) olive oil

Wash duck and cut into pieces; pat dry with towel. Set aside liver, heart and gizzard. In skillet brown duck pieces in heated oil. Arrange duck pieces in baking dish. Add bay leaves, salt, pepper and wine. Bake uncovered in 350°F (180°C) oven, basting occasionally for 1 3/4 hours or until tender.

Meanwhile, make the sauce: Chop gizzard and heart. Add 1 cup (250 ml) water. Bring to boil, lower heat and simmer for 15 minutes. Cut prosciutto and liver into small pieces and sauté in olive oil for 4 minutes. Add chopped gizzard, heart and their broth and cook until liver is dissolved, about 10 minutes.

Pour liver sauce over cooked duck and bake an additional 15 minutes. Lay duck on heated platter. Skim and discard fat from remaining sauce and pour over duck. Serve immediately.

Serves 4
Suggested wine: Chianti,
Brunello di Montalcino,
Vino Nobile di Montepulciano

ANATRA ALLA SALSA PICCANTE
Spicy Duck Treviso Style

1 whole duck, about 4 pounds (2 kg)
4 tablespoons (60 ml) butter
4 slices bacon, chopped
3 fresh sage leaves, chopped, or 1/4 teaspoon (2 ml) crushed dried sage
1 sprig fresh rosemary, chopped, or 1/4 teaspoon (2 ml) crushed dried rosemary
1 lemon, cut in half
Salt and freshly ground black pepper to taste

LA SALSA PICCANTE
THE SPICY SAUCE
4 tablespoons (60 ml) butter
1 garlic clove, crushed
2 tablespoons (30 ml) chopped fresh parsley
1 whole bay leaf
1/4 pound (125 g) cooked shrimp
1/4 teaspoon (2 ml) coarsely ground fresh black pepper
2 anchovy fillets, chopped
1/2 cup (125 ml) red wine vinegar

Wash duck and pat dry with towel. Save the giblets and liver for something else. With fork prick duck skin all over. In large ovenproof casserole melt butter. Add bacon, sage and rosemary and sauté 5 minutes. Add duck, lemon halves, salt and pepper and sauté a few minutes more. Put uncovered casserole in preheated 425°F (220°C) oven. After about 30 minutes skim and discard most of the fat in the casserole. With a fork prick skin of duck to help melt the fat. Continue roasting until duck is tender and browned, basting with its juices as necessary, for about 30 more minutes.

In separate skillet prepare the sauce: Melt the butter, add garlic, parsley, bay leaf, chopped shrimp and pepper. Sauté until lightly browned. Add anchovies and vinegar and cook until vinegar is half evaporated. Take casserole out of the oven. Pour sauce inside duck cavity and all over body and return casserole to oven. In 5 minutes turn off oven but leave duck inside for 25 more minutes before serving.

Serves 4
Suggested wine: Barbera,
  Rubesco

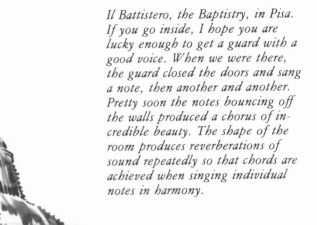

Il Battistero, the Baptistry, in Pisa. If you go inside, I hope you are lucky enough to get a guard with a good voice. When we were there, the guard closed the doors and sang a note, then another and another. Pretty soon the notes bouncing off the walls produced a chorus of incredible beauty. The shape of the room produces reverberations of sound repeatedly so that chords are achieved when singing individual notes in harmony.

The powerful tower in the Palazzo della Signoria in Florence, as seen from the Piazza degli Uffizi.

At the base of the Palazzo there is a grandiose fountain done by the sculptor Bartolomeo Ammannati. I was told that somewhere around the fountain there was a small plaque with the inscription Ammannato, Ammannato, che bel marmo hai rovinato, *which means "Ammannato, Ammannato, what beautiful marble you have ruined" and was supposed to have been put there by the sculptor's friends, in jest. I spent a lot of time looking for it but never found it. Maybe the jest was on me.*

Verdure
Vegetables

The rich soil of Northern Italy produces a great variety of vegetables, and Italians are very particular when it comes to selecting the youngest, freshest and most perfect specimens for their dishes.

Steamed or boiled vegetables are usually served as a *contorno,* or accompaniment to meat or fish. More intricate vegetable dishes, of amazing variety and creativity, are generally served as a separate course to be fully appreciated by themselves.

SPINACI AL LIMONE
Spinach with Lemon

This dish combines three ingredients in which Florence, the dominant city of the region of Tuscany, excels: *spinaci, limone, e olio d'oliva.* Anything cooked with *spinaci* automatically receives the title of Florentine. The cooks of Florence do indeed have a magic touch with spinach. Florentines have experimented with hybrids of lemons and oranges since olden days producing some amazing combinations. And there doesn't seem to be a table where lemons are not served for one dish or another.

When Tuscans give you a recipe and they tell you to add *olio buono,* good oil, they mean olive oil. Genoans of the neighboring region of Liguria boast of their excellent local oil. But a Florentine cook told me, with typical regional pride, that he suspects that when they make their famous *pesto alla genovese,* they secretly use the olive oil from his Tuscany. The reason for the quality difference, he said, is that during the harvest, the Ligurians allow the olives to fall to the ground. In Tuscany, however, the ground under the trees is covered with cloths or war surplus parachutes, so that the olives, upon falling, never touch the ground.

1 bunch spinach for every two
   people
Lemons, cut into wedges
Olive oil

Wash spinach under cold running water. Drain. Cook in covered pot with no more water than clings to the leaves, or cook in steamer for only a couple of minutes so it is barely wilted. Drain and chill in refrigerator. Cut through spinach one or two times and serve in individual dishes with a wedge of lemon. Tactfully direct your guests to pour olive oil on the spinach first and then plenty of lemon juice. No salt is necessary.

Serve with no wine

SPINACI CON ACCIUGHE
Spinach with Anchovies

The Piedmontese serve this dish sprinkled with croutons. Crisp bacon bits may be sprinkled over it also. All in all, though, I prefer my *spinaci con acciughe* straight. Do not add salt as the anchovies are salty enough.

4 pounds (2 kg) spinach
4 tablespoons (60 ml) butter
1 whole garlic clove
4 anchovy fillets, mashed
Dash freshly ground black
    pepper

Rinse spinach, shake to drain and cook in covered pot, with only the water clinging to the leaves, for 5 minutes. Drain thoroughly and set aside. In skillet melt butter and sauté garlic until pale gold, not brown. Take out and discard garlic. Add anchovies and mix well with butter. Cut through spinach once or twice and add to butter mixture. Add pepper. Cook until spinach is hot and *insaporito* or flavored.

Serves 4
Serve with no wine

CAVOLFIORE CON SALSA DI ACCIUGHE
Cauliflower with Anchovy Sauce

When you come to the table with a whole cauliflower on a platter garnished with this rich sauce you are bound to make an impression upon *famiglia e amici,* family and friends. When I was testing this recipe on my husband, I asked him, "Will one whole cauliflower serve four people?" "No," he said, "only one." So you see, the impression is not only visual.

1 large cauliflower
1 cup (250 ml) water
4 anchovy fillets
1/4 pound (125 g) butter
2 tablespoons (30 ml) chopped
    fresh parsley
1/8 teaspoon (1 ml) crushed dried
    hot pepper (optional)
1 lemon, cut into wedges

Rinse whole cauliflower. Remove hard part of stem and large green leaves. Leave the small leaves on. Put it whole in steamer or in large pot on a trivet to keep cauliflower from touching water. Add water. Cover and steam for 10 minutes or until tender but still firm.

While cauliflower steams make the sauce: Remove as many spines from anchovies as are visible. Crush anchovies to a paste. In small saucepan melt butter, turn off burner, add anchovies, parsley and hot pepper. Mix well. Put hot cauliflower on heated platter. Pour sauce over. Serve immediately and offer lemon to squeeze over cauliflower. Platter may also be garnished with a ring of cooked young potatoes or carrots with butter.

Serves 4
Serve with no wine

COTOLETTE DI ASPARAGI ALLA PAVESE
Breaded Asparagus Pavia Style

2 pounds (1 kg) asparagus
2 eggs, beaten
Salt to taste
Dried bread crumbs
$^1/_4$ pound (125 g) butter

Rinse asparagus; break off and discard tough white parts. With cotton string tie asparagus into a bundle with tips in one direction. Stand the bundle upright in a deep narrow pot with boiling water to cover the lower tougher ends of the asparagus. The tips are out of the water and will get steamed not boiled. Cover pot and cook for 15 minutes or until asparagus are tender but still firm. Drain, then cool in refrigerator until ready to serve. Dip each asparagus in egg with salt, dust all over with crums and in skillet sauté in melted butter. Serve immediately.

Serves 4
Suggested wine: Pinot, Trebbiano

ASPARAGI ALLA FIORENTINA
Asparagus Florentine Style

2 pounds (1 kg) asparagus
$^1/_4$ pound (125 g) butter
Freshly ground black pepper to taste
$^1/_2$ cup (125 ml) freshly grated parmesan cheese
4 eggs

Rinse asparagus, break off and discard tough white parts. With cotton string tie asparagus into a bundle with tips in one direction and cook them upright in deep narrow pot with water to cover lower tougher ends of asparagus. Cover pot and cook 15 minutes so asparagus are still firm. Drain and dry with towel. In skillet sauté them in some of the butter. Arrange in heated platter; sprinkle with pepper and grated parmesan. Fry eggs in remaining butter and put them over asparagus. Serve immediately.

Serves 4
Suggested wine: Same wine as for the main dish

Small statue in the Museo dell'Opera del Duomo, Florence

BROCCOLI E CAVOLFIORE ALLA MILANESE
Broccoli and Cauliflower
Milan Style

2 pounds (1 kg) broccoli
1 cauliflower, about 2 pounds
   (1 kg)
Butter for sautéeing as needed
1 teaspoon (5 ml) cold-pressed
   sesame oil or corn oil
1/4 cup (60 ml) flour
2 or 3 eggs, beaten
1/2 cup (125 ml) dried bread
   crumbs

1/2 cup (125 ml) freshly grated
   parmesan cheese
2 lemons, quartered

Remove leaves and trunk from broccoli and cauliflower. Peel broccoli trunk and cut into bite-sized pieces. Discard all leaves and trunk of cauliflower. Cut rest of vegetables into flowerettes, rinse and cook uncovered in boiling salted water until just firm or *al dente.* (The broccoli trunks will take a couple of minutes longer so you may want to put

them in ahead of the flowerettes.) Drain and allow to cool thoroughly.

In skillet melt 2 tablespoons (30 ml) butter over medium heat with oil. Dust a few vegetable pieces at a time with flour, or shake them with flour inside a paper bag. Dip them in beaten eggs, then in mixture of crumbs and parmesan cheese. Sauté in butter until golden. Repeat process for each batch adding butter as needed. Keep warm until all are fried. Serve right away with quartered lemons.

Serves 4 to 6
Suggested wine: Same wine as
   main course or a dry white
   wine

SEDANO ALLA MILANESE
Celery Milan Style

2 large or 4 small bunches of
   celery
2 tablespoons (30 ml) butter
1 tablespoon (15 ml) flour
1 cup (250 ml) warm beef broth,
   page 30
2 tablespoons (30 ml) brandy
4 fresh mushrooms, sliced
1 tablespoon (15 ml) freshly
   grated parmesan cheese
1 tablespoon (15 ml) dried bread
   crumbs
2 teaspoons (10 ml) butter for
   topping

Fifteenth-century terracotta in the
Casa Bagatti-Valsecchi, Milano

Remove coarse outer stalks from celery (use them for soup). Rinse celery in cold water. Cook uncovered in boiling salted water for 5 minutes. Drain thoroughly. Lay them on buttered baking dish, not much bigger than celeries lying side by side.

Now prepare the sauce: In saucepan melt butter. Add flour and stir until brown. Add broth a little at a time as you mix with a wire whisk and cook, stirring until smooth, even and thickened, about 5 minutes. Remove from fire and add brandy. Place mushroom slices on top of celery and cover with the sauce. Sprinkle with mixture of parmesan and bread crumbs and dot with pieces of butter. Bake in preheated 350°F (180°C) oven for 30 minutes or until golden.

Serves 4
Suggested wine: Same wine as main course or a dry white wine

ZUCCHINE RIPIENE
Stuffed Italian Squash

2 pounds (1 kg) whole zucchini
1 cup (250 ml) ricotta cheese
1 cup (250 ml) chopped leftover cooked meat
2 eggs
Salt and freshly ground black pepper to taste
1/2 cup (125 ml) freshly grated parmesan cheese
1/4 cup (60 ml) dried bread crumbs
2 tablespoons (30 ml) chopped fresh parsley
Butter

Wash zucchini and in uncovered pot cook with boiling water until half cooked, about 5 minutes. Cut zucchini lengthwise in half, carefully scoop out centers making canoes out of them. Set the canoes aside. In a bowl mash the zucchini you scooped out. Add rest of ingredients, except butter, and mix well. Stuff the zucchini canoes with the mix. (If you have leftover mix stuff a scooped-out tomato or green pepper.) Lay the stuffed zucchini on buttered baking dish. Sprinkle zucchini with additional bread crumbs and dot with little pieces of butter on top. Bake in preheated 400°F (210°C) oven for 20 minutes or until top is golden brown.

Serves 4
Suggested wine: Same wine as the main dish. If served by itself: Orvieto, Frascati

ZUCCHINE FRITTE
Fried Zucchini

This recipe comes from Elba, the beautiful island off the Tuscan coast. To make *zucchine fritte alla milanese,* or Milan style, omit salt, add 1/2 cup (125 ml) freshly grated parmesan cheese to the bread crumbs, fry in butter with only a teaspoon of oil and serve with plenty of lemon wedges.

2 pound (1 kg) zucchini
1/4 cup (60 ml) flour, approximately
1 or 2 eggs, beaten
Salt to taste
1/2 cup (125 ml) dried bread crumbs
Cold-pressed sesame oil or corn oil

Wash and dry zucchini. Cut them into slices, dip them in flour, then into beaten eggs mixed with salt and then into bread crumbs. In skillet sauté them immediately in hot oil.

Serves 4
Suggested wine: Same wine as for the main dish

MELANZANE ALLA PARMIGIANA
Eggplant in the Style of Parma

My husband has never been partial to eggplant. So when I was testing this recipe he wasn't particularly looking forward to supper. When I brought the dish to the table and showed it to him, I asked how many people did he think the amount would serve. He looked at it and answered, "Thirty." After we polished off the whole thing, he commented, "I guess it will serve only two gluttons, but four people."

Melanzane alla parmigiana is messy to prepare. It uses lots of pots and lots of oil, but it is worth it, especially for people who think they don't like eggplant. I tried an experiment that reduces the amount of oil considerably and produces a reasonable facsimile: Broil the eggplants until they are black all over. Peel and slice them and use in layers with the sauce and other stuff as called for in the recipe. But now I will give you the traditional method.

4 eggplants, about $^1/_2$ pound (225 g) each
3 tablespoons (45 ml) butter
3 tablespoons (45 ml) chopped onion
1 garlic clove, chopped
$14^1/_2$-ounce (410 g) can italian-style tomatoes or 1 pound (500 g) peeled and seeded fresh tomatoes
2 fresh basil leaves, chopped, or $^1/_4$ teaspoon (2 ml) crushed dried basil
Salt and freshly ground black pepper to taste
1 cup (250 ml) olive oil
$^1/_4$ cup (75 ml) freshly grated parmesan cheese
6 slices bacon, crisply fried, or equivalent amount of fried prosciutto, crumbled
8 ounces (225 g) mozzarella cheese, sliced
2 tablespoons (30 ml) dried bread crumbs
1 teaspoon (5 ml) butter

Peel eggplants, cut into finger-thick slices and soak in salted water for 45 minutes. If you put a weight on them the slices will stay below the water. Soaking keeps the eggplant from absorbing too much oil during frying.

In the meantime prepare the sauce: In deep skillet put butter, onion and garlic and sauté until pale gold, not brown. Add

Detail of the Allegory of November, Battistero in Parma

chopped tomatoes and basil. Simmer for about $1/2$ hour. When cooked, process in blender or pass through colander. Add salt and pepper.

Dry eggplant slices with towel. In skillet heat plenty of olive oil and fry eggplant on both sides. If you press down with your spatula it will brown more quickly and evenly. Drain eggplant on absorbent paper.

In buttered deep baking dish put a layer of fried eggplant. Sprinkle with parmesan cheese then crumbled bacon or prociutto. Put layer of mozzarella, spoon layer of sauce evenly over and start with eggplant again. Keep layering until you end with eggplant. Spoon last of sauce and sprinkle with bread crumbs. Dot with specks of butter and bake in preheated 350°F (180°C) oven for about 45 minutes. Serve hot.

Serves 4
Suggested wine: Lacrima Cristi Bianco, Ischia Bianco, Corvo Bianco

FAGIOLI
Beans

In the old days, when beans were still called *fagiuoli,* after the bread had been baked in the *forno da campagna* or country oven, the beans would be cooked very slowly in the remaining heat. In our energy-conscious times we could be using the heat remaining in our ovens after baking to start a pot of beans. Italians are fond of using young beans or haricots, which are more tender and require less cooking.

FAGIOLI NEL FIASCO
Beans in a Bottle

Fiasco in Italian means bottle or flask, not a disaster. These beans, famous in Tuscany, are made, as the name tells, in a large bottle, right on the coals of a charcoal brazier. The bottle must be left open and be big enough so the beans have room to swell.

2 cups (500 ml) dried white beans
9 cups (2.25 L) water
$1/4$ cup (60 ml) olive oil
1 fresh sage sprig
1 garlic clove
2 slices thick bacon, cut in pieces or, piece salt pork
Salt and freshly ground white pepper to taste
1-gallon (4 L) size clean empty wine bottle

Wash beans and soak overnight in water. Start coal fire burning in brazier. Put beans, soaking water, olive oil, sage, garlic, bacon, salt and pepper in bottle. Set bottle in bowl of warm water to warm up the glass. Dry bottle thoroughly with towel. Place uncapped bottle directly on bed of coals and allow beans to simmer for 2 hours or until tender. Beans should have enough water still in bottle to allow for ease of pouring. When cooked, pour out beans, remove sage and garlic.

Serves 6
Suggested wine: Chianti

Window along a street in Florence

FAGIOLI ALL'UCCELLETTO
Beans in the Style of Little Birds

This Florentine dish is also called *fagioli a guisa d'uccellini,* beans disguised as little birds, which describes the actual fact that the beans are cooked in the same manner as a dish prepared with little birds. Sometimes fresh haricot or young beans are used, which need no soaking, in which case they are cooked in boiling water for a much shorter time than dry beans. *Fagioli all'uccelletto* is served as a *contorno* or side dish to meat, especially boiled beef.

1 pound (500 g) dried white
    beans
Salt to taste
1/4 cup (60 ml) olive oil
1 garlic clove, crushed
3 fresh sage leaves, chopped, or
    1/2 teaspoon (5 ml) crushed
    dried sage
Freshly ground black pepper to
    taste
4 fresh tomatoes, without skins
    or seeds

Rinse beans and soak in water overnight. In uncovered pot cook beans in soaking water very slowly, until tender. Add salt about halfway during cooking.

In casserole make a *soffritto,* or sauce, by sautéeing in oil, garlic and sage until garlic is just blond, not brown. Add drained beans and pepper and cook until beans are nicely flavored. Chop tomatoes, pass through sieve and add to the beans. Add salt if needed. Cook 10 more minutes, at most, and serve.

Serves 6
Suggested wine: Chianti, or same
   wine as main course

LENTICCHIE IN UMIDO
Lentil Stew

1 pound (450 g) lentils
1/8 pound (50 g) thick bacon
   slices, chopped
3 tablespoons (45 ml) butter
2 tablespoons (30 ml) finely
   chopped onion
2 tablespoons (30 ml) finely
   chopped carrot
2 tablespoons (30 ml) finely
   chopped celery stalk
14 1/2-ounce (410 g) can italian-
   style peeled tomatoes, drained,
   or 1 pound (500 g) peeled
   fresh plum tomatoes
Hot water as required
1 beef bouillon cube
Salt and freshly ground black
   pepper to taste

Rinse lentils and soak in water overnight. In heavy pot put bacon, butter, onion, carrot and celery and sauté about 5 minutes. Drain lentils (save the soaking water), add lentils to pot and sauté another couple of minutes. Add tomatoes. Add salt, pepper, the saved soaking water and bouillon cube. Cook uncovered over very low burner. Add hot water a little at a time as needed until lentils are still whole yet tender and the sauce is rich not watery.

Serves 4
Suggested wine: Trebbiano,
   Orvieto

CARCIOFI CON LE PATATE
Artichokes with Potatoes

Dishes of this type where vegetables are cooked in tomato sauce are called *alla contadina* or *alla campagnola,* or country style.

10 small artichokes
1 lemon
2 large potatoes

1/4 cup (60 ml) olive oil
1 garlic clove, cut in half
1 small onion, chopped
1 cup (250 ml) tomato sauce,
   see page 62
1/4 teaspoon (2 ml) salt
1/4 teaspoon (2 ml) freshly
   ground black pepper
1 cup beef broth, page 30
1 pinch dried sweet basil

Remove hard outer leaves of artichokes down to the tender edible ones. Cut stems and tips off artichokes. Rinse well and cut in half lengthwise. Soak them in water with juice of lemon for 5 minutes. Take them out and allow to drain. Peel and cube potatoes, soak them in the lemon water.

In casserole heat oil and sauté garlic until blond; remove and discard garlic. Add onion, drained and dried potatoes and artichokes. Sauté a few minutes. Add tomato sauce and remaining ingredients. Bring to a boil, cover, lower temperature and simmer for 30 minutes or until artichokes are tender.

Serves 4
Suggested wine: Frascati,
   Verdicchio

SFORMATO DI FINOCCHIO
Fennel Mold

This is an aromatic dish served as *contorno* or vegetable accompaniment to a meat dish.

1 head fennel, about 1 pound (500 g)
3 tablespoons (45 ml) butter
3 tablespoons (45 ml) flour
1 cup (250 ml) milk
2 tablespoons (30 ml) freshly grated parmesan cheese
1 pinch salt
3 eggs, beaten
2 tablespoons (30 ml) dried bread crumbs

Remove harder outer leaves of fennel and trim base. Cut into pieces. Cook in salted water for 20 minutes or until tender. Drain. Chop cooked fennel very fine or pass through a sieve. In skillet, sauté fennel in butter 5 minutes. Add flour, mixing well. Then stir in milk a little at a time. Cook until smooth and thickened. Remove from fire and allow to cool. Add parmesan and salt. Little by little, add eggs, mixing very thoroughly. Pour into buttered tube pan. Sprinkle with crumbs. Set tube pan in another pan containing 2 inches (5 cm) water. Bake in preheated 400°F (210°C) oven for 20 minutes or until top is golden and inserted toothpick comes out clean. Serve immediately.

Serves 6
Suggested wine: Torgiano Bianco, Pinot Bianco, Orvieto

Feline statue on top of pilaster in the façade of the Cathedral in Pisa

Dolci e Pasticcerie
Desserts and Pastries

Northern Italians generally complete their meals with cheese and fruit, but have a penchant for rich desserts and pastries which they savor between meals, when entertaining and on other special occasions.

When I was gathering recipes in Italy, I wanted to reciprocate the generosity of the people, so I always offered some of my own recipes in return for theirs. More often than not, they would express polite indifference to salty dishes but would perk up with interest and attention if the recipe was for dessert.

WINES AND DESSERTS

With desserts it is usual to serve sweet wines of high alcohol content, spumantes, or sparkling wines, or sweet liqueurs. Many pastries in fact, already contain a liqueur, and in such cases it is best to serve a similar one to avoid a contrast of tastes. Asti Spumante is perhaps the only exception, since it can accompany any kind of dessert. Marsala both sweet and dry is also versatile and can be served in the majority of cases. Drier desserts such as sweet breads would find a suitable accompaniment in wines such as Moscato or Passito.

Except for Asti Spumante which must be served chilled, it is advisable to serve dessert wines at room temperature, if not a few degrees warmer. Some people might disagree on this point. The most fascinating aspect about wines is that *one* truth does not exist. So feel free to experiment and trust your own judgement.

FRAGOLE CON PANNA
Strawberries and Cream

Florentines adore fresh strawberries. For them there seems to be no better way to end a good lunch than savoring, very slowly, a dish of *fragole con panna*.

1 basket strawberries, about 3/4 pound (350 g)
Juice of 1 lemon
1/2 pint (250 ml) whipping cream
1 1/2 tablespoons (25 ml) sifted powdered sugar

Remove stems from strawberries. Wash strawberries in running cold water (do not soak). Drain and set them in a bowl. Sprinkle with lemon juice and allow to rest 5 minutes. Separately whip cream and sugar until stiff. Drain strawberries; reserve 4 most beautiful for garnish. Serve in well-chilled glass cups with whipped cream on top, capped by the lush berry.

Serves 4
Suggested wine: Crema Marsala, Amaretto

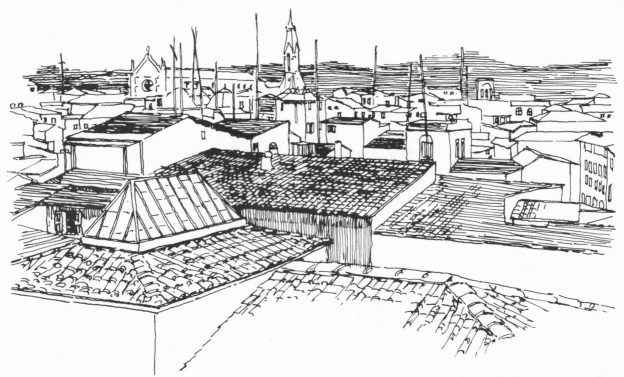

Rooftops of Florence as seen from the window of the Galleria degli Uffizi, the museum in the Uffizi Palace

MELONE AL MARSALA
Melon with Marsala Wine

Incidently, the cantaloupe is named from the castle of Cantalupo in Italy where it was first grown in Europe.

2 cantaloupes
1¹/₂ tablespoons (25 ml) sugar
¹/₂ cup (125 ml) Marsala wine
4 scoops vanilla ice cream, or
 ¹/₂ pint (250 ml) whipping cream
4 strawberries

Cut cantaloupes in half. Remove seeds and filaments. With scooping spoon or knife take out most of flesh in small balls or cubes leaving enough on skin so it holds its shape. In bowl, put melon pieces. Add sugar and wine. Fill empty melon shells with mixture. Chill well and serve, with a scoop of ice cream or a dollop of whipped cream over, and a strawberry on top.

Serves 4
Suggested wine: Crema Marsala

La Rocca, Assisi, a medieval fortress, as seen from the town

MACEDONIA
Mixed Fruit Delight

2 cantaloupes
Assorted fruit in season: sliced
   bananas, orange slices, sliced
   peaches, grapes, etc.
3 tablespoons (45 ml) sugar
1 cup (250 ml) Marsala wine

Cut cantaloupes in half. Remove
seeds and filaments. With scooping spoon or knife take out most
of flesh in small balls or cubes
leaving enough on skin so it
holds its shape. In bowl, put
fruit pieces. Add sugar and wine.
Fill empty melon shells with mixture. Serve well chilled.

Serves 4 or more
Suggested wine: Amaretto

ZABAGLIONE
Wine Custard

4 egg yolks
4 tablespoons (60 ml) sugar
1 pinch salt
Small piece lemon peel
3/8 cup (100 ml) Marsala wine
1 tablespoon (15 ml) rum
   (optional)

In bowl beat yolks with sugar
and salt until light yellow, thick
and fluffy. Add lemon peel and
put mixture in top of double
boiler. Make sure water under is
not boiling but only simmering.
Beating with wire whisk, add
wine and rum very gradually.
Continue beating until it
thickens. Remove lemon rind.
Zabaglione should come out fluffy and smooth. Serve hot or cold
in stemmed glasses. If you serve
it cold, stir before serving
because it separates. Some people
like to add a dash of cinnamon
on top or serve with a cookie.

Serves 4
Suggested wine: Crema Marsala

ZUCCOTTO
Cheese and Brandy Icebox Cake

While talking with Dr. Giovanni
Parenti in Siena, he told me that
his family had owned a pharmacy
and had been manufacturing
panforte, a typical Sienese fruit-
cake, for over one hundred years.
Apparently *panforte* was always
made by pharmacists. While talking about traditional dishes he
told me a story of how *zuccotto*
came to be.

According to the story, during
one of the many wars of the
Renaissance, soldiers stored their
food supplies packed in snow inside caves, to keep them cold
during the warm months. The
salt from the walls allowed the
snow to become colder without
turning into ice. One day some
wine happened to spill on the
cold snow turning it into a sort
of spiked sherbet. One of the
soldiers, an architect by the name
of Buontalenti, who as his name
implies, was not lacking in
talent, took a taste of the stuff
and said, "This is good! And if
it's good with wine, why not
with something else." So the
soldiers removed their metal
scull-caps or *zucchetti* and in
them mixed the cold snow with
all kinds of sweet and tasty
things. And so, Buontalenti from
his *zucchetto*, the soldiers from
their *zucchetti* happily ate their
zuccotto.

Zuccotto today is one of the
favorite desserts in Florence and
is made by lining glass bowls
with a pound cake and filling it
in various sweet ways, from
vanilla to chocolate, from ice
cream to whipped cream, or from
pudding to cheese. You can use
store-bought pound cake, but if
you have time to make your own
it is well worth it.

Statue of Sant'Alessio and diamond pattern stonework on the Church of Santa Trinita in Florence. The facade of this Romanesque building was done in the sixteenth century by the architect Buontalenti.

ZUCCOTTO DI RICOTTA
Ricotta Cheese and Brandy Cake

THE POUND CAKE
6 eggs
3/4 cup (175 ml) sugar
1 tablespoon (15 ml) water
1 pinch salt
Juice and grated rind of 1/2
    lemon
2/3 cup (150 ml) flour
1/3 cup (75 ml) potato starch or
    cornstarch

In large bowl beat eggs, sugar, water and salt until very light and fluffy. Beat in lemon juice and rind. In another bowl sift flour and starch together. Gently, and a little at a time, fold the flour and starch mixture into egg mixture. Do not mix or overwork. Butter a baking pan, line bottom with wax paper and butter top of paper also. Pour in batter and bake in preheated 350°F (180°C) oven for 40 minutes or until golden and a

Prophet Elia, San Geminiano, Modena

toothpick inserted into middle comes out clean. Allow to cool 10 minutes before unmolding. Let cool completely before using in the *zuccotto*.

BUILDING THE ZUCCOTTO
1 pound cake, preceding
1/2 cup (125 ml) brandy
1/2 cup (125 ml) sweet liqueur
    such as Aleatico, Maraschino or
    Sweet Marsala
1/2 pint (250 ml) whipping cream
1/2 pound (250 ml) ricotta cheese
6 tablespoons (90 ml) sifted
    powdered sugar
1 pinch salt
1 1/2 teaspoons (7 ml) vanilla extract (powder is better than
    liquid)

Line 2 glass bowls 6 inches (15 cm) in diameter with 1/2 inch (1.5 cm) thick slices of pound cake sprinkled with mixture of brandy and liqueur. In separate bowl, whip cream until stiff. In another bowl whip ricotta with sugar, salt and vanilla. Fold whipped cream and ricotta mixture together. Fill cake-lined bowls with mixture and refrigerate overnight. To serve turn over on a plate and cut into wedges at the table.

Serves 8
Suggested wine: Strega,
*   Amaretto*

ZUCCOTTO GELATO
Ice Cream Cake

This version of *zuccotto* is a favorite at Florence bar-coffee shops.

1 pound cake, preceding
1/2 cup (125 ml) rum
1/2 cup (125 ml) sweet liqueur
    like Aleatico, Maraschino or
    Sweet Marsala
1 quart (1 L) spumoni ice cream,
    or vanilla ice cream mixed with
    1/2 cup (125 ml) chopped
    candied fruit
1 quart (1 L) chocolate ice cream
1/4 cup (60 ml) coarsely chopped
    walnut meats
1/4 cup (60 ml) coarsely grated
    bittersweet chocolate

Line 2 glass bowls 6 inches (15 cm) in diameter with slices of pound cake sprinkled with mixture of rum and liqueur. Fill to half with spumoni or vanilla ice cream mixed with candied fruit. Fill the rest with mixture of chocolate ice cream, walnuts and chocolate bits. Keep covered in freezer until serving time, but not less than 3 hours. Turn over on chilled plate and slice at the table.

Serves 8
Suggested wine: Amaretto,
*   Sambuca*

ZUPPA INGLESE
Brandy and Custard Cake

Zuppa inglese translates literally to "English soup." Since it is actually a trifle, I can only speculate that the name is a subtle commentary on the English. Some people use rum instead of brandy, others use *biscotti savoiardi,* lady fingers, or store-bought pound cake instead of making the *pane di spagna,* sponge cake. All of which illustrates that Italians don't hesitate to modify a recipe.

PANE DI SPAGNA
SPONGE CAKE
6 egg yolks
3 egg whites
1 1/4 cups (300 ml) sugar
1/8 teaspoon (1 ml) salt
Grated rind of 1/2 lemon
1 1/2 cups (375 ml) flour, sifted
1/4 pound (125 g) butter, melted

In top of double boiler put yolks, whites, sugar and salt. Beating with wire whisk, heat until lukewarm. Remove from heat and continue beating until very frothy, about 10 minutes. Add lemon rind. Without beating or stirring fold in flour a little at a time. Fold in butter. Pour into a buttered and floured 8-inch (20 cm) round pan, approximately 2 1/2 inches (6 cm) deep. Bake in preheated 325°F (160°C) oven for 1 hour or until golden brown and toothpick inserted in center comes out clean. Allow to cool on wire rack.

CREMA PASTICCERA
PASTRY CUSTARD
2 eggs
2 egg yolks
1 cup (250 ml) sugar
1/4 teaspoon (2 ml) salt
2 1/2 tablespoons (40 ml) flour
2 cups (500 ml) milk
1/2 vanilla pod, or 1 teaspoon
    (5 ml) vanilla extract

In bowl put eggs, yolks, sugar and salt. Mix with wire whisk. Separately mix flour with milk and add to egg mixture. Add vanilla, put mixture in saucepan and set over low fire. Keep mixing and cook, without allowing it to boil, until thickened. Let cool.

UN PO' DI TUTTO
ODDS AND ENDS
1/2 cup (125 ml) apricot jam
1/2 cup (125 ml) brandy
1 pint (500 ml) whipping cream
3 tablespoons (45 ml) sifted
    powdered sugar
1/3 cup (75 ml) finely chopped
    citron, figs, apricots or other
    dried fruits

In cup mix jam and brandy. In separate chilled bowl, whip cream and sugar until stiff (stop before you make butter). Now you are ready to put the *zuppa* together.

CONSTRUCTING THE ZUPPA
Carefully cut sponge cake into three layers. Put one layer on platter and sprinkle with one-third brandy mixture. Cover with layer of half of the custard. Sprinkle with one third of candied fruit. Put on second cake layer. Sprinkle with one-third brandy mixture, rest of custard and another third candied fruit. Put on last layer of cake and sprinkle with remaining brandy mixture. Apply whipped cream over top and sides with pastry bag and ornamental nozzle. Arrange remaining candied fruit over cream in an artistic pattern.

Serves 6
Suggested wine: Crema Marsala,
    Asti Spumante

Detail on the north doors of the
Baptistry in Florence. These doors
were done by Ghiberti, who also did
the famous Doors of Paradise on the
east side of the building.

DOLCE AL MASCARPONE
Coffee and Cream Dessert

Mascarpone is a creamy, soft cheese made in Lombardy and Tuscany, used in all kinds of great desserts. Since we have nothing like it in the States, I've experimented with different combinations and found that cream cheese and whipping cream turn out a convincing facsimile. If you happen to be visiting Italy and want to make this recipe, use $3/4$ pound (375 g) *mascarpone* and omit the cream cheese and whipping cream. I've arranged the whipping so you don't have to keep washing your beaters.

$1^1/2$ tablespoons (25 ml)
    powdered instant coffee
1 cup (250 ml) hot water
2 eggs, separated
$1/2$ pint (250 ml) whipping cream
8 ounces (250 g) cream cheese
4 tablespoons (60 ml) sugar
4 tablespoons (60 ml) rum
7-ounce (200 g) box *biscotti savoiardi* or lady fingers or cat's tongues, page 162
2 tablespoons (30 ml) coarsely grated bittersweet chocolate

Dissolve coffee in hot water. Set aside to cool. In bowl, beat egg whites until stiff. In another bowl, whip the cream until stiff. In yet another and larger bowl beat cream cheese and sugar until fluffy and smooth. Beat in one egg yolk at a time. Mix in half the rum. Fold the whipped cream and egg whites gently into cheese mixture. To the coffee add the rest of the rum. Dip *biscotti* in coffee-rum mixture and place a layer in bottom of deep glass baking dish. Cover with a layer of cheese mixture and sprinkle with some chocolate bits. Next put a layer of dipped *biscotti,* and so on in alternating layers ending with cheese mixture ornamented with chocolate bits. Cover and freeze until firm but not hard, about 1 or 2 hours. Then refrigerate until serving.

Serves 4 to 6
Suggested wine: Vin Santo

BUDINO DI GIULIA
Piedmontese Pudding

$3/4$ cup (175 ml) sugar
24 *biscotti* or lady fingers or cat's tongues, page 162
$1^1/2$ cups (350 ml) Marsala wine
6 eggs, beaten
$1/4$ cup (60 ml) crushed amaretti (almond flavored cookies)
$1/4$ cup (60 ml) bitter cocoa
2 tablespoons (30 ml) Curaçao, or other fine liqueur
2 cups (500 ml) milk
6 tablespoons (90 ml) sugar

Put the $3/4$ cup sugar in 2-quart (2 L) ovenproof bowl and place in 350°F (180°C) oven. When sugar melts (watch it does not burn), spread to cover sides and bottom of bowl. Set aside to cool. Soak *biscotti* well in Marsala and with them line inside of sugar coated bowl. Mix eggs, amaretti, chocolate, Curaçao, milk and the remaining sugar. Pour into bowl slowly so you don't disturb the *biscotti.* Bake in preheated 375°F (190°C) oven for 30 minutes. When cool, invert pudding onto serving plate.

Serves 8
Suggested wine: Caluso Passito, Passito di Pantelleria

CRÈME CARAMELLE ALLA ROBERTO
Baked Custard

Instead of using plain milk and sugar I have taken liberties and substituted evaporated and condensed milk, but since my Florentine friend Roberto Guerrini did not object, this recipe still bears his name.

1/2 cup (125 ml) brown sugar
2 eggs
4 egg yolks
13-ounce (397 g) can sweet condensed milk
13-ounce (397 g) can evaporated milk
1/8 teaspoon (1 ml) salt
1 teaspoon (5 ml) vanilla extract

Put sugar in a tube pan. Set in 400°F (210°C) oven until sugar melts. With wood spoon spread melted sugar all over inside. Set aside to cool. In bowl mix, without beating, eggs and yolks. Mix in milks, salt and vanilla. Pour mixture into sugar coated pan. Place pan in baking dish containing 1 inch (3 cm) water and bake in preheated 450°F (230°C) oven for 20 to 30 minutes, or until a toothpick inserted into custard comes out clean. Let cool, loosen edges with point of knife, put serving plate over and turn upside down.

Serves 6 to 8
Suggested wine: Crema Marsala

SOFFIATO DI CIOCCOLATO
Chocolate Soufflé

6 tablespoons (90 ml) sifted powdered sugar
1/4 cup (60 ml) grated sweet chocolate
1 teaspoon (2 ml) vanilla extract
5 egg yolks
2 cups (500 ml) milk
5 egg whites

In small saucepan beat well the sugar, chocolate, vanilla and egg yolks. Add milk. Place on low heat. Cook until thick, stirring constantly. Allow to cool for 15 minutes. Beat egg whites until very stiff. Fold whites gently into chocolate mixture. Pour into generously buttered soufflé dish or other high, straight-sided baking dish. Bake near top of preheated 375°F (190°C) oven for 30 minutes. Serve immediately, otherwise soufflé will sadly collapse.

Serves 6
Suggested wine: Asti Spumante

CREMA AL CAFFÈ
Coffee Mousse

1 pint (500 ml) whipping cream
3 tablespoons (45 ml) sifted powdered sugar
1 pound (500 g) ricotta cheese
1/2 teaspoon (2 ml) fresh lemon juice
2 tablespoons (30 ml) instant coffee dissolved in
2 teaspoons (10 ml) hot water
3 tablespoons (45 ml) brandy
1 cup (250 ml) coffee liqueur
Mandarin orange slices (optional)

In bowl whip cream with 1 tablespoon (15 ml) sugar until soft peaks form. Separately combine ricotta, the remaining sugar, lemon juice, dissolved coffee, the brandy and half the liqueur. Beat until smooth. Gently blend three-fourths whipped cream into cheese mixture. Into well-chilled dessert glasses distribute the remaining liqueur, fill with cheese mixture, top with drained fruit and a puff of whipped cream.

Serves 8
Suggested wine: Brandy, Grappa, Sambuca

TORTA CON CREMA DI BIANCA
Piedmontese Cake with Chocolate Frosting

3 egg yolks
6 tablespoons (90 ml) sugar
1 1/2 tablespoons (25 ml) flour
2 cups (500 ml) milk
1/4 cup (60 ml) grated bittersweet
 chocolate
Pane di Spagna (sponge cake),
 page 141
Dry Marsala wine

In saucepan beat egg yolks and sugar. Blend in flour. Add milk very slowly, mixing well. Add chocolate. Put saucepan on low heat and cook, stirring constantly, until mixture begins to thicken. Continue cooking, 5 minutes more, stirring and raising up mixture with spoon (this makes for slower cooking process).

Slice sponge cake in half, making two layers. Sprinkle Marsala wine on cut surfaces of the two layers. Spread half the frosting on one layer and cover with second layer. Spread remaining frosting on top surface of cake.

Serves 6
Suggested wine: Asti Spumante,
 Moscato di Pantelleria

TORTA DI PESCHE ALLA PANNA
Peaches and Cream Cake

The sight of round shiny peach halves in a fluffy bed of whipped cream is a dessert eater's delight.

8 eggs
1 1/4 cup (300 ml) sugar
2 cups (500 ml) flour
1 teaspoon (5 ml) vanilla extract,
 or grated rind of 1 lemon
1/4 teaspoon (2 ml) salt
4 tablespoons (60 ml) melted
 butter
1 pint (500 ml) whipping cream
2 tablespoons (30 ml) powdered
 sugar
1 16-ounce (500 g) can peach
 halves, drained
3/4 cup (175 ml) syrup from
 peaches
3/4 cup (175 ml) rum

Statue in the Museo dell'Opera del Duomo, Florence

In top of double boiler put eggs and sugar; heat while beating until lukewarm. Remove from fire and continue beating until frothy and increased to twice its volume. Add flour, vanilla or lemon rind, salt and butter, folding gently. Butter a 9-inch (23 cm) cake pan. Line bottom with wax paper. Butter top of wax paper and dust with flour the entire inside. Pour batter into pan and bake in preheated 350°F (180°C) oven for 50 to 60 minutes or until golden brown and a toothpick inserted into middle comes out clean. Remove cake from oven, turn upside down on rack to cool. Peel off wax paper from cake.

In bowl, whip cream and sugar until stiff. When cake is cold cut into 2 or 3 round layers. Sprinkle each with mixture of peach syrup and rum. Build up cake by alternating layers of cake and whipped cream. On top of last layer of cake place drained peaches round side up. With pastry bag and ornamental tip distribute whipped cream between peaches and over sides of cake. Keep refrigerated until serving time.

Serves 8
Suggested wine: Crema Marsala,
 Vin Santo

STIACCIATA FIORENTINA
Florentine Carnival Cake

Carnevale is the equivalent of the carnival or Mardi Gras of New Orleans. It is celebrated in the period preceding Lent, and it ends on the Tuesday before Ash Wednesday. *Carnevale* is a time for games, jokes and merry-making. People dress up in masks and costumes based mainly on characters of literature and folklore. Many of the foods eaten are deep fried because, like Mardi Gras or fat Tuesday in French, *Carnevale* is a fat event.

1 tablespoon (15 ml) active dry
   yeast
1 1/4 cups (300 ml) warm water,
   110°F (50°C)
6 cups (1.5 L) flour
1 whole egg
2 egg yolks
1/2 teaspoon (2 ml) salt
1/2 cup (125 ml) sugar
Grated rind of 1 orange or lemon
3/8 pound (175 g) softened butter
Sifted powdered sugar

Dissolve yeast in water. Place 4 cups (1 L) flour on board. Make well in center. Pour yeast dissolved in warm water into well. Mix and knead until smooth, about 5 minutes, adding more water or flour if needed until dough is pliable and no longer sticky. Put dough in buttered bowl. Turn to grease top. Cover with damp cloth. Allow to rest in warm place free of drafts until doubled in bulk, about 1 hour. An oven with pilot light is a good spot. Or, set pan with hot water at bottom of unheated oven and place bowl with dough on rack near the top. When dough has risen, uncover and punch down. Add beaten eggs, salt, sugar and grated rind. Work it well together. Place 1 cup (250 ml) flour on board. Put dough over and knead, dusting with flour as needed until dough is no longer sticky. Add butter and knead until well incorporated. Gather and place over remaining flour and knead until dough is smooth, pliable and no longer sticky. Form 2 equal balls and press flat and evenly into two buttered and floured pans, 9x12 inches (23x30 cm). Allow to rise uncovered in a warm place 1 hour or until doubled in bulk. Bake in preheated 400°F (210°C) oven 20 or 30 minutes until golden brown. Cool on a rack.

Remove from pan and dust with sifted powdered sugar. Slice to serve.

Serves 8
Suggested wine: Vin Santo

SCHIACCIA BRIACA
Drunken Flat Cake

Schiaccia briaca is said to originate from the small village of Capoliveri, on the island of Elba. Capoliveri is perched at the top of a flower-covered hill which dips steeply to the sea. The center of town is the spot where six crooked streets come together. The resulting small contained space serves as a depot for cars, the bus and delivery trucks. It serves as pedestrian plaza, outdoor café, a vending place for fresh fish, vegetables and clothes as well as stage setting for the daily interactions among the townspeople. There are the school children on their way to school, garbed in their blue checkered aprons. There are the dogs that belong to no one in particular. There is the grandiose and robust policeman, uniformed and fully armed, who is treated more as a relative than a cop, and who probably is. And at one corner, advertising the local bank there stands the fancy clock that displays unchangingly 12:45.

Schiaccia briaca is served during *Il Natale*, Christmas, and other festive occasions.

2 cups (500 ml) flour
3/4 cup (175 ml) sugar
1 1/2 teaspoons (7 ml) baking powder
1/8 teaspoon (1 ml) salt
Grated rind of 1/2 lemon
1/4 cup (60 ml) corn oil
1/2 cup (125 ml) Moscato wine
3 tablespoons (45 ml) pine nuts
1/2 cup (125 ml) seedless raisins

In bowl mix all ingredients, saving some of the pine nuts and raisins to decorate the top later. When dough is blended save a piece to make ornaments. Place rest of dough in a buttered and floured 10 inch (25 cm) round pan. Make a long rope out of the piece of dough you saved and write words or make designs as you please. Use pine nuts and raisins creatively, enjoy yourself. Bake in preheated 375°F (190°C) oven for 45 minutes or until toothpick inserted into middle comes out clean. *Schiaccia* should be dark outside and dry inside.

Serves 8
Suggested wine: Vin Santo, Asti Spumante

*Cattedrale di San Rufino, Assisi,
1140–1200 AD. The square is used
by children to play soccer.*

TORTA DI NOCI E CEDRO
Nuts and Citron Cake

3/8 pound (150 g) shelled walnuts
1 1/3 cups (325 ml) sifted
    powdered sugar
1 1/3 cups (325 ml) bitter cocoa
1 teaspoon (5 ml) vanilla extract
1/2 cup (125 ml) finely chopped
    candied citron
4 egg yolks, beaten
4 egg whites
1/2 cup (125 ml) seedless raisins
1/2 cup (125 ml) brandy

In large mortar or large bowl, crush walnuts and mix with sugar. Add cocoa, vanilla, citron and beaten egg yolks. With fingers, crumble so there are no large lumps and all is sort of cornmealy. Separately whip egg whites until stiff but not dry. Add 4 tablespoons (60 ml) of the beaten whites to the nut mixture to moisten it, then fold in the rest, gently so you don't flatten the whites. Butter a 9-inch (23 cm) round or square baking pan and dust it with mixture of half flour, half powdered sugar. Pour batter into baking pan and bake in preheated 350°F (180°C) oven for 30 minutes or until a toothpick inserted into center comes out clean.

Now, you may think you are finished, but the best part is yet to come. Take cake and crumble it into a bowl and add raisins and brandy. Gather it into a ball and shape it into a compact long brick. Wrap the *torta* in wax paper and store a couple of hours or longer, before serving.

Serves 4 to 6
Suggested wine: Caluso Passito,
*   Passito di Pantelleria*

PIZZA RICOTTA
Cheese Pie

THE DOUGH
2 1/4 cups (525 ml) flour
2 hard-boiled egg yolks
2 raw egg yolks
1 teaspoon (5 ml) baking powder
1/2 teaspoon (2 ml) salt
1 1/2 cups (350 ml) sifted
    powdered sugar
3/8 pound (175 g) butter
1 tablespoon (15 ml) water
Grated rind of 1 orange

THE FILLING
1 pound (500 g) ricotta cheese
6 egg yolks
1/2 teaspoon (2 ml) salt
Grated rind of 1 orange
1 cup (250 ml) loosely filled,
    white seedless raisins
2 tablespoons (30 ml) chopped
    candied citron or candied
    orange peel
1 cup (250 ml) sugar

On wood board pile flour. In well, formed in center, add rest of dough ingredients. Mix the contents of well until blended then incorporate the flour without working it too much. Make a ball and let rest.

In bowl mix ricotta with rest of filling ingredients until well blended. Set aside. On floured board roll dough into a large flat circle. With it line bottom and sides of buttered and floured pan about 10 inches (25 cm) in diameter and 1 1/4 inches (4 cm) high. Cut off part of dough that hangs over edge of pan and save for ornaments. Fill with ricotta mixture. Roll out dough remnants and cut into hearts, leaves, or what have you. Paint them with beaten egg and place over ricotta mixture. Bake in preheated 375°F (190°C) oven for 45 minutes or until a knife inserted into middle comes out clean. Remove from oven, sprinkle with powdered sugar and allow to cool.

Serves 8
Suggested wine: Lacrima Cristi
*   Dolce, Moscato d'Asti*

TORTA DI ANANAS
Pineapple Cake

This handsome coffeecake makes use of the versatile *pasta frolla* or short pastry, and *confettura,* fruit preserves.

LA PASTA FROLLA
THE SHORT PASTRY
2 1/2 cups (600 ml) flour
3/8 pound (175 g) butter at room temperature
1/2 teaspoon (2 ml) baking soda
6 tablespoons (90 ml) sifted powdered sugar
4 egg yolks
1/2 teaspoon (2 ml) salt
1 1/2 tablespoon (25 ml) Marsala wine
1 egg, beaten, for glazing the finished pastry (optional)

Sift flour onto a wood board. Make a crater in center and in it put all other ingredients except last egg. Incorporate everything quickly. Do not overwork. Make into 2 balls, one twice as large as the other. Place them between sheets of wax paper and refrigerate 15 minutes.

LA CONFETTURA DI ANANAS
THE PINEAPPLE PRESERVES
8-ounce (225 g) can unsweetened crushed pineapple
1/2 cup (125 ml) sugar

In saucepan bring pineapple with its juice and sugar to a boil. Keep boiling for 8 minutes stirring occasionally. It is ready when juice spilled from a spoon drips two droplets at the same time, instead of one at a time, when the spoon is almost empty.

BUILDING THE TORTA
Leaving large ball of *pasta frolla* between wax papers, roll it into flat circle big enough to cover and slightly overhang a pie pan. Remove one wax paper, ease dough into buttered and floured pie pan, dough side down. Fit gently, remove other wax paper and trim excess all around. Ornament edge by pinching. Fill with pineapple fruit preserve. Incorporate the trimmed pieces of dough into the remaining ball of dough. Roll without wax paper on floured board and cut into ornamental shapes such as stars, circles, strips or whatever. Lay shapes over fruit preserve and paint with beaten egg if you want a glossy surface. Bake in preheated 400°F (210°C) oven for 18 minutes or until light gold. Cool before serving.

Serves 8
Suggested Wine: Crema Marsala

TORTA DI MARZAPANE
Marzipan Cake

MARZIPAN FILLING
4 1/2 ounces (130 g) canned almond paste
1 cup (250 ml) sifted powdered sugar
1 tablespoon (15 ml) butter
1 tablespoon (15 ml) finely chopped candied citron
1 egg yolk
1 teaspoon (5 ml) almond extract

Pasta frolla, preceding recipe

Mix all filling ingredients until well blended. Set aside.
Make a *pasta frolla* according to preceding recipe. Roll large ball of dough between sheets of wax paper until you have a circle 10 inches (25 cm) in diameter. Remove one wax paper. Place dough side down in center of buttered and floured cookie sheet. Remove other wax paper. Take a piece from the remaining dough and make a finger-thick rope. Press rope on top of pastry around edge of circle to form a rim. Spread marzipan filling evenly to the rim. On floured board roll remainder of dough. Cut into fancy cookie shapes which you arrange over the marzipan. Paint entire surface with

beaten egg if you want a glossy surface. Bake in preheated 350°F (180°C) oven for 20 minutes or until light gold. Cool before serving.

Serves 8
Suggested wine: Crema Marsala

TARTELETTE DI FRUTTA ALLA MILANESE
Fruit Tarts Milan Style

THE PASTRY
$2^{1}/4$ cups (525 ml) flour
$3/8$ pound (175 g) butter at room temperature
5 tablespoons (75 ml) sugar
3 egg yolks
$1/4$ teaspoon (1 ml) salt
$1/4$ teaspoon (1 ml) baking soda
Grated rind of 1 lemon
2 tablespoons (30 ml) Marsala wine

THE FILLING
2 tart apples, peeled and sliced
2 pears, peeled and sliced
16-ounce (454 g) can sour cherries, drained
Sifted powdered sugar
Salt

THE GLAZE
$1/2$ cup (125 ml) apricot jam
2 tablespoons (30 ml) rum

Sift flour into a bowl. With pastry blender cut in butter until it looks like coarse meal. Add sugar, egg yolks, salt, soda, rind and Marsala and working quickly, blend into a smooth dough. Make a ball, wrap in wax paper and refrigerate 30 minutes. On floured surface roll thin, cut into circles and ease each one into a muffin tin or tart mold overlapping edge slightly. Pinch or crimp all around to make a fluted rim. Fill some with apples, some with pears and some with cherries. Sprinkle $1/2$ tablespoon (8 ml) powdered sugar and pinch salt over each one. Bake in preheated 350°F (180°C) oven for 30 minutes or until dough is lightly browned. Remove from oven. In small saucepan heat apricot jam, mix with rum and brush mixture over fruit in tarts. Allow to cool before unmolding.

Makes 8 to 12 tarts
Suggested wine: Asti Spumante

Casa degli Omenoni, Milano

Desserts and Pastries 151

BIGNOLINE E CANNONI RIPIENI
Èclairs with Pastry Custard

When these pastry puffs are round shaped, they are called *bigne* when big, *bignoline* when small. If they are long shaped they are know as *cannoni* or cannons. They can be stuffed with whipped cream sweetened with a bit of powdered sugar, or *crema pasticcera,* pastry custard. Tops can be left plain or glazed with powdered sugar dissolved with a bit of hot water and sprinkled with grated chocolate. Or dip tops of èclairs in melted chocolate.

ÈCLAIR DOUGH
1 cup (250 ml) water
6 tablespoons (90 ml) butter
1 pinch salt
1 cup (250 ml) flour
4 eggs

In saucepan bring water, butter and salt to a boil. Add flour all at one time, stirring continually over low heat. Cook 2 minutes. Remove from heat and allow to cool. Beat in one egg at a time, waiting until each is completely incorporated before adding the next. Using a pastry bag with a large round nozzle, extrude round gobs 1 inch (3 cm) in diameter, and also finger-shaped gobs 1 inch by 2 1/2 inches (3 by 8 cm), on a clean cookie sheet. Bake in preheated 450°F (230°C) oven for 15 minutes. Reduce heat to 250°F (120°C) and continue baking 15 more minutes. Remove from oven and allow to cool thoroughly. Fill hollow inside with pastry custard (following) or sweetened whipped cream, using a pastry bag. Leave top plain or glaze with topping.

CREMA PASTICCERA
PASTRY CUSTARD
2 eggs
3 egg yolks
2/3 cup (160 ml) sifted powdered sugar
1/2 teaspoon (2 ml) salt
3 tablespoons plus 1 teaspoon (50 ml) flour
2 cups (500 ml) lukewarm milk
1/3 piece vanilla bean, or small piece lemon peel, or 1 teaspoon (5 ml) vanilla extract

In bowl, beat eggs, yolks, sugar and salt for 10 minutes. Add flour. Then milk a bit at a time. Add vanilla or lemon peel and butter. In saucepan heat mixture to simmer; do not allow to boil. Continue cooking, stirring continually until thickened. You'll know custard is ready if the edge of the spoon leaves a slight ridge on the surface when you make a cutting motion on it. Chill before using to stuff pastry.

Variations: Add dissolved instant coffee or a bar of bittersweet chocolate during cooking.

Serves 4 to 6
Suggested wine: Crema Marsala

The more you look at the façade of San Marco in Venice, the more hidden figures seem to appear, like this little trumpet player perched on one of the friezes.

Desserts and Pastries   153

PASTA SFOGLIA
Puff Pastry

This dough is best made during cool dry weather and when you have about three hours to spare. With it you can make all sorts of flaky pastries such as *cornucopie* or cornets, page 158; *sfogliatine storte*, crooked pastries, page 157; *sfogliatelle*, flaky pastries with custard, page 157; and *millefoglie*, thousand layer cake, page 157.

There are a few tricks you should know before you start that will make life easier. When you roll the dough at first, there will probably appear small air bubbles. Prick them carefully with a toothpick. When rolling the dough always do it up and down, never sideways, except when it's ready to be used. At that time you will extend it by rolling in all directions. Use as little flour as possible to dust board, and clean board and rolling pin each time before you start rolling the dough. Whenever setting dough to rest, put wax paper under and over and make sure it is in a cool place. If the dough is to be stored, wrap well in wax paper and refrigerate. When you take it out, let it sit at room temperature a while otherwise it will crack if you try rolling while it's hard.

4 cups (1 L) flour
1 pound (500 g) butter, cut into bits and chilled
3/4 cup (175 ml) water, mixed with
1/4 teaspoon (2 ml) salt

Using pastry cutter or fingers mix 1 cup (250 ml) flour with butter. Make a compact square patty. Cover with cloth and leave in cool place or refrigerate 15 minutes. Mix remaining flour with enough salted water to make a smooth pliable dough. Knead well, hitting it like a whip against the board. This flogging makes the dough more elastic and relieves any pent-up feelings of aggression. Make a square patty. Cover with cloth and chill in refrigerator 15 minutes. Now begin the folding business.

Step 1. On lightly floured board roll dough made of flour and salted water into large square about half a finger thick. In center place butter dough patty. Fold left third over center, then right third over center. Now fold bottom third over center. Flip the whole thing over like a page in a book. Then fold upper third toward you, over the center, resulting in a "Z" fold. Chill in refrigerator 15 minutes.

Step 2. On barely floured surface place dough so the edges of the layers are toward you. With rolling pin roll up and down into a rectangle half a finger thick. Fold in thirds by bringing upper third over center then lower part over center. Chill in refrigerator 15 minutes.

Step 3. On barely floured board, turn dough 90 degrees so edges of layers are toward you again. Roll into rectangle. Fold in fourths by bringing upper edge down to center, then lower edge up to center and then upper part over lower. Chill in refrigerator 15 minutes.

Step 4. Repeat step 2. Let rest 45 minutes. The dough is now ready to be used.

PASTA SFOGLIA RAPIDA
Quick Puff Pastry

Even though this pastry dough is not as splendid as the elegant *pasta sfoglia*, preceding, neither does it take three hours to make. Pastries made with the quick version are quite good. An added advantage is that you do not require cool weather to get a satisfactory result. Use this dough in any recipe calling for *pasta sfoglia*.

3 cups (700 ml) refrigerated flour
$^1/_8$ teaspoon (1 ml) salt
1 pound (500 g) chilled butter
1 tablespoon (15 ml) fresh
    lemon juice
$^3/_4$ cup (175 ml) chilled water

In large chilled bowl put flour,
salt and butter. Using pastry
blender or two knives, cut butter
into the flour until it looks like
wheat kernels or small peas. Add
lemon juice mixed with water.
Mix quickly with spoon, gathering it into a ball. Put on lightly
floured board and with rolling
pin roll into long rectangle. Fold
bottom third up and then top
third down. Turn 90 degrees so
open end, where you can count 3
layers, is toward you. Roll up and
down into rectangle again. Now
fold bottom third up then top
third down. Turn 90 degrees and
repeat process for a total of 6
times. Remember always to roll
up and down only, toward the
open ends. Never toward the
folded edges, except when you
are ready to extend the dough
for cutting at which time you roll
in all directions. If you must
abandon dough for any length of
time, refrigerate it until you are
ready. When you take it out of
the refrigerator let it sit at room
temperature a while, otherwise it
will crack if you try rolling while
it's hard.

*Panel depicting the Nativity in the
bronze door of San Ranieri in the
Cattedrale or Cathedral, in Pisa*

Palazzo Comunale or Town Hall,
Perugia. Between the Palazzo and
the Cattedrale di San Lorenzo stands
the Fontana Maggiore, an ornate,
many-pillared fountain by Nicola
and Giovanni Pisano.

SFOGLIATINE STORTE
Flaky Crooked Pastries

When you have leftover pieces of *pasta sfoglia*, page 154, or *pasta sfoglia rapida*, page 154, cut them into short strips about the size of a finger. Twist them like a cork-screw and lay them on cookie sheet dampened with water. In small saucepan put 1/2 cup (125 ml) apricot, pineapple or other fruit jam and 2 tablespoons (30 ml) hot water. Cook and stir a few minutes. With pastry brush coat tops of *storte* with jam mixture. Sprinkle them with coarse sugar or mixture of coarse sugar and ground blanched almonds. Bake in preheated 400°F (210°C) oven for 10 minutes or until brown and crisp.

Suggested wine: Asti Spumante

SFOGLIATELLE
Flaky Pastries with Custard

Ingredients for *pasta sfoglia*, page 154, or *pasta sfoglia rapida*, page 154
Ingredients for *crema pasticcera*, page 152, or *crema di cioccolata*, page 160
Sifted powdered sugar

Prepare 1 recipe *pasta sfoglia* or *pasta sfoglia rapida*. On lightly floured board and using light even pressure of the rolling pin, roll out dough into large circle 1/8 inch (3 mm) thick. With sharp knife and without dragging the blade, cut into 3-inch (8 cm) squares. Cut squares at the diagonal to make 2 equal triangles, (or using sharp cookie cutter cut into circles). Lay them on cookie sheet dampened with water. Prick pastry with fork a few times. Bake in preheated 450°F (230°C) oven for 12 minutes or until brown and crisp. Allow to cool.

Build up the *sfogliatelle* by putting *crema* between layers of triangles. You can also split the baked shapes into 2 or more layers and put the *crema* between each layer. Dust tops with sifted powdered sugar.

Serves 12
Suggested wine: Asti Spumante

MILLEFOGLIE
Thousand Layer Cake

Ingredients for *pasta sfoglia*, page 154, or *pasta sfoglia rapida*, page 154
Ingredients for *crema pasticcera*, page 152
3 tablespoons (45 ml) Marsala wine
1/2 cup (125 ml) apricot preserves
Sifted powdered sugar

Prepare 1 recipe *pasta sfoglia* or *pasta sfoglia rapida*. On lightly floured board and using light even pressure of the rolling pin, roll out dough into large square, 1/8 inch (3 mm) thick. With sharp knife and without dragging the blade, cut into 4 equal squares. Place them on dampened cookie sheets. Prick all over with fork and bake in preheated 450°F (230°C) oven for 12 minutes or until brown and crisp. Allow to cool. Prepare the *crema pasticcera* and allow to cool. Lay one layer of pastry on platter. Spoon over it as much *crema* as it will hold. Cover with second layer of pastry. Sprinkle with Marsala. Spoon *crema* over and cover with third layer. Smear preserves on and cover with fourth layer. Then cover top with sifted powdered sugar.

Serves 8 to 12
Suggested wine: Amaretto, Galliano

CORNUCOPIE
Cornets or Horns of Plenty

To make these handsome, professional-looking pastries you will need six or twelve cornet molds. These metal cones are available where kitchen accessories are sold.

Ingredients for *pasta sfoglia*, page 154, or *pasta sfoglia rapida*, page 154
1 egg, beaten
Sifted powdered sugar

Prepare 1 recipe *pasta sfoglia* or *pasta sfoglia rapida*. On lightly floured board and using light even pressure of the rolling pin, roll out dough into large circle 1/8 inch (3 mm) thick. With a sharp knife and pressing down with blade, not dragging it, cut dough into 1-inch (3 cm) wide strips. Dampen cornet molds with water and beginning at pointed end wind a strip of dough around each one, overlapping each turn slightly over the one beneath. Lay molds on their sides on cookie sheet dampened with water; make sure the free end of dough is facing down. Brush tops with beaten egg. Bake in preheated 450°F (230°C) oven for 12 minutes or until brown. Take out, sprinkle with powdered sugar and return to oven for an additional 2 minutes. Allow to cool before unmolding. Using a pastry bag fill each pastry cone with whipped cream, as follows, or with *crema pasticcera*, page 152, or *crema di cioccolata*, page 160.

PANNA MONTATA
WHIPPED CREAM
1 pint (500 ml) whipping cream
1/4 cup (60 ml) sifted powdered sugar
1/2 teaspoon (3 ml) vanilla extract

In chilled bowl whip all ingredients together until stiff.

Serves 12
Suggested wine: Crema Marsala, Asti Spumante

BRUTTI MA BUONI
Ugly But Good Cookies

No self-respecting bakery in Florence would omit *brutti ma buoni* from its inventory. The cookies do not always taste the same at different bakeries. Nor for that matter, do they always taste the same at the same bakery at different times. Nor are they always unusually ugly, but they always taste good.

1 pound (500 g) blanched almonds
2 cups (500 ml) sifted powdered sugar
1 tablespoon (15 ml) apricot jam
1/2 teaspoon (2 ml) vanilla extract
1/2 teaspoon (2 ml) almond extract
1 pinch salt
2 egg whites
1/4 cup (60 ml) crushed walnuts

With mortar and pestle or blender, crush almonds to a paste. Mix in sugar, jam, vanilla and almond extract and salt. Mix in egg whites except for 2 teaspoons (10 ml) which you set aside. When well blended, put mixture on floured board and make balls about 1 inch (3 cm) round. Flatten them slightly, brush tops with reserved egg white and sprinkle with walnuts. Arrange on buttered and floured baking sheet. Bake in preheated 350°F (180°C) oven for 18 minutes or until light brown.

Makes about 2 dozen cookies
Suggested wine: Asti Spumante

Rhinoceros, detail from the bronze doors of the Cathedral in Pisa, eleventh to thirteenth century. In *1515 Albrecht Dürer did a woodcut which is almost identical to this rhino. If you go to Pisa, stand on the walk joining this door of the* *Cathedral and the Baptistry. The feeling of perfect symmetry on that spot is almost overwhelming.*

PASTINE DA BAGNARE
Italian Dunking Cookies

Dunking your cookies in hot chocolate, coffee or tea is not only not frowned upon in Italy, it is positively encouraged by concocting tough little biscuits you would be hard put to eat straight. Each region has its own version of *pastine da bagnare*, or dunking cookies. The Piedmontese have their *biscotti duri* or hard biscuits, and the Venetians have their long lasting *baìcoli* and also their *focaccia*, medieval hearth cake.

8 eggs
2 cups (500 ml) sugar
2 cups (500 ml) flour
1 tablespoon (15 ml) aniseed
2 cups (500 ml) sliced walnuts or
   blanched almonds

Beat eggs 5 minutes. Add sugar, beating well. Add flour and continue beating. Mix in aniseed and nuts. Pour into 2 greased and floured bread pans. Bake in preheated 350°F (180°C) oven for 1 hour. Remove from oven and cut into 1-inch (3cm) slices. Return to 150°F (60°C) oven for 1 more hour.

Makes about 1 1/2 dozen cookies
Sugested wine: Crema Marsala

Desserts and Pastries   159

PASTINE DI MARMELLATA
Cookies with Preserves

These delicate cookies from the region of Romagna will melt in your mouth.

1/4 pound (125 g) butter, at
    room temperature
2 1/2 tablespoons (40 ml) sugar
2 eggs, separated
1/4 teaspoon (2 ml) fresh lime
    juice
1/4 teaspoon (2 ml) freshly grated
    lime rind
1/8 teaspoon (1 ml) salt
1 cup (250 ml) flour
Apricot or strawberry preserves
1/2 cup (125 ml) walnut meats

Beat butter and sugar until fluffy. Beat in egg yolks one at a time. Add lime juice, rind and salt. Mix in flour until well blended. Make balls 1 inch (3 cm) round. Dip them in egg white and place them on buttered and floured cookie sheet. With your finger make a slight depression in center of each ball and fill with bit of fruit preserves. Insert a few small pieces of walnut around the fruit. Bake in preheated 400°F (210°C) oven for 15 minutes.

Makes about 2 dozen cookies
Suggested wine: Vin Santo,
    Lambrusco Dolce

PASTINE DI MARZAPANE
Marzipan Cookies

The procedure is the same as for *pastine di marmellata*, preceding, but instead of filling centers with fruit preserves, use the following marzipan. Also, omit the walnut garnish.

MARZIPAN FILLING
4 1/2 ounces (125 g) blanched
    almonds
3/4 cup (175 ml) sifted powdered
    sugar
1 tablespoon (15 ml) butter
1 tablespoon (15 ml) finely
    chopped candied orange peel
1 egg yolk
1 teaspoon (5 ml) almond extract
1 tablespoon (15 ml) water

With mortar and pestle or in blender mash all ingredients together until you have a smooth paste. If too dry add bits of water until it is no longer crumbly.

Makes about 2 dozen cookies
Suggested wine: Crema Marsala,
Moscato di Siracusa

BACI DI DAMA
Lady's Kisses

These little pastries are made of two delicate cookies, stuffed with a rich chocolate cream. They literally melt in your mouth.

CREMA DI CIOCOLATA
CHOCOLATE CREAM

Crema di cioccolata can also be used to stuff *cornucopie*, page 158, or when making *sfogliatelle*, page 157, both of which are made with the many-layered *pasta sfoglia*. You can make this cream using 2 eggs and 3 yolks but the more yolks the more delicate the result.

1 egg
5 egg yolks
1 cup (250 ml) sugar
4 ounces (125 ml) bittersweet
    chocolate, grated
2 1/2 tablespoons (35 ml) flour
1 teaspoon (5 ml) vanilla extract
Small piece yellow part of lemon
    peel
1 quart (1 L) milk

In bowl mix egg, yolks, sugar, chocolate, flour and vanilla until well blended. Add lemon peel and milk. In saucepan over low fire, cook mixture, gently mixing with wire whisk, until thickened. Cook a bit longer. Remove lemon peel and set cream aside to cool. Discard or eat the film that forms on the surface.

COOKIES FOR BACI DI DAMA

$^1/3$ pound (150 g) butter, at
 room temperature
$^3/4$ cup (175 ml) sugar
$^1/4$ teaspoon (2 ml) salt
3 eggs, beaten
1 teaspoon (5 ml) brandy
$^1/4$ teaspoon (2 ml) freshly grated
 lemon rind
Juice of $^1/2$ lemon
$^1/2$ teaspoon (3 ml) vanilla extract
$1^1/2$ cups (350 ml) cornstarch
1 cup (250 ml) flour
$^1/2$ teaspoon (3 ml) baking
 powder

In bowl beat butter until fluffy.
Beat in sugar and salt, then the
eggs, gradually. In separate bowl
mix brandy, lemon rind, juice
and vanilla. In yet a separate
bowl sift together cornstarch,
flour and baking powder. Now,
to the butter mixture add alter-
nate amounts of the brandy mixture and the flour mixture until
well blended. Allow to rest 30
minutes. On board dusted with
cornstarch roll dough about
$^1/2$-inch ($1^1/2$ cm) thick. Cut
small rounds. Gently transfer
them to clean cookie sheet and
bake in preheated 325°F (160°C)
oven for 20 minutes or until pale
gold. Cool and fill between pairs
of rounds with *crema di cioccolata.*

Makes 3 to 4 dozen cookies
Suggested wine: Asti Spumante

*View through wrought-ironwork on
top of Pauline Rock, Perugia. In the
center you can see the Chiesa di San
Ercolano, or Church of St. Herculan.
While you are in Perugia, you must
taste their chocolate and candy, it is
the finest in the world.*

LINGUE DI GATTO
Cats' Tongues

$1/4$ pound (125 g) butter, at
    room temperature
1 cup (250 ml) sifted powdered
    sugar
$1/4$ teaspoon (2 ml) salt
2 egg whites
1 cup (250 ml) flour
1 teaspoon (5 ml) vanilla
    extract

In bowl beat butter, sugar and
salt until fluffy. Add 1 egg
white, mixing well. Mix in half
the flour and then the other egg
white. Add remaining flour and
vanilla and blend well. On barely
buttered cookie sheet, using a
pastry bag equipped with a plain
tip, shape batter into long
fingers, or I should say, cats'
tongues. Allow room between for
them to grow during baking.
Bake in preheated 375°F (190°C)
oven until lightly golden, about
15 minutes.

Makes about 2 dozen cookies
Suggested wine: Asti Spumante,
    Caluso Passito

BUGIE DI ELSA
Piedmontese Deep Fried Cookies

Why these pastries are called
bugie, or "lies," no one could
tell me. As a break from sight-
seeing, all over Italy, tourists
gather at small windows where
vendors display deep-fried
pastries of all kinds, similar to
the Piedmontese *bugie.* Most
sightseers in Italy are Italians,
who are untiring admirers of
their innumerable treasures.

4 egg yolks
$1 1/2$ teaspoons (7 ml) vanilla or
    almond extract
2 cups (500 ml) flour
$1/4$ teaspoon (2 ml) salt
Cold-pressed sesame or corn oil
    for deep-frying
Granulated sugar

Beat eggs very well. Add extract.
Sift in flour and salt, a little at a
time, beating well, until mixture
is too stiff to continue. Turn onto
floured board. Knead until very
smooth, using additional flour as
needed to prevent sticking.
Divide dough into small sections.
On floured board with rolling
pin, roll until very thin. Using
ravioli cutter or kitchen knife, cut
into strips $1 1/2$ inch (4 cm) wide.
Cut diagonally some strips into
pieces 3 inches (8 cm) long. Cut
other strips into pieces 6 to 8
inches (15 to 20 cm) long to be
then tied into a single knot. In
skillet, heat oil until very hot.
Deep-fry a few cookies at a time,
moving them around until they
are golden brown on both sides.

During cooking, each cookie will
swell and twist, taking on its own
personality. Remove from oil and
drain on paper towels. Sprinkle
immediately with granulated
sugar. *Bugie* are especially good
eaten as soon as cool. Store ex-
tras, when thoroughly cooled, in
airtight containers.

Makes about 4 dozen cookies
Suggested wine: Vin Santo

FRATI AL BURRO
Friars in Butter

These pastries come from the
island of Elba. They are called
friars because their doughnut
shape is, with some stretch of the
imagination, somewhat reminis-
cent of a friar's head with its
round bald spot.

1 tablespoon (15 ml) active dry
    yeast
1 cup (250 ml) lukewarm water
4 cups (1 L) flour
1 tablespoon (15 ml) sugar
3 tablespoons (45 ml) butter, at
    room temperature
Corn oil for deep-frying
Sifted powdered sugar

Dissolve yeast in lukewarm water.
Put flour on board and make a
crater in center. Put sugar and
dissolved yeast in crater and

begin to incorporate flour, adding more lukewarm water if necessary to make a firm, pliable dough. Knead until quite elastic. Work butter into dough and knead until smooth. Allow to rest 20 minutes, covered with a cloth. On floured board roll dough about 3/8 inch (1 cm) thick. Cut into circles and from each circle cut a smaller circle or use a doughnut cutter if you have one. In deep-fryer, heat oil and fry the friars a few at a time until golden brown on both sides. Take them out and dip them in powdered sugar. Serve hot or cold.

Makes about 4 dozen doughnuts
Suggested wine: Vin Santo

FRITTELLE DI RISO CON LATTE
Rice and Milk Fritters

3/4 cup (175 ml) long-grain white rice
2 cups (500 ml) milk
1 tablespoon (15 ml) butter
1 tablespoon (15 ml) sugar
1/4 teaspoon (2 ml) salt
1 teaspoon (5 ml) freshly grated orange rind

2 tablespoons (30 ml) brandy or rum
3 eggs, separated
1/2 cup (125 ml) flour
Cold-pressed sesame oil or corn oil for frying
Sifted powdered sugar

In uncovered heavy pan, over medium heat and without boiling, cook rice in milk with butter, sugar, salt and orange rind until rice is slightly overdone. Allow to cool. Mix in liqueur and egg yolks, one at a time. Then mix in flour. Keep covered in refrigerator for 2 hours. Beat whites until stiff and gently fold into rice mixture. In skillet fry immediately by spoonfuls in hot oil until brown on both sides. Dip in powdered sugar and serve hot.

Serves 4 to 6
Suggested wine: Crema Marsala

FRITTELLE DI CARNEVALE
Carnival Fritters

These fritters are served in Florence during the Carnival festivities in February.

1 cup (250 ml) flour
1/2 teaspoon (2 ml) salt
1/3 cup (100 ml) dry white wine

2 tablespoons (30 ml) grappa or brandy
1 egg, separated
1 1/3 cup (350 ml) long-grain white rice
2 2/3 cups (700 ml) water
Salt
1 teaspoon (5 ml) baking powder
Corn oil for frying
Granulated sugar

In bowl mix flour, salt, wine, grappa and egg yolk. Beat egg white until stiff; fold into flour mixture. Allow to rest while you prepare the rice. In pot put rice and lightly salted cold water. Bring to boil, lower temperature and simmer uncovered for 17 minutes, until almost tender. Rinse rice well, then drain. Add baking powder into flour-egg mixture and blend with cooked rice. Baking powder must not be allowed to rest or the *frittelle* will not rise. In skillet heat oil until very hot. Drop mixture by spoonfuls and fry until brown on both sides. Drain on absorbent paper and then roll in sugar to coat all over. Let cool.

Serves 4 to 6
Suggested wine: Vin Santo

Index

APPETIZERS AND SALADS
Bagna Cauda, 25
Chicken Livers on Toast, 24
Crab in its Shell, 20
Crescents Bologna Style, 26
Fennel and Tomato Salad, 15
Marinated Fresh Anchovies, 21
Mixed Salad, 15
Old Bread Salad, 18
Oysters Gratinée, 22
Piedmontese Fondue, 26
Piedmontese Hot Dip, 25
Prawns Venetian Style, 22
Raw Fava Beans, 15
Rice Salad, 17
Scampi, see Prawns
Squid and Celery Salad, 19
Wilted Cabbage Salad, 17

SOUPS AND BROTHS
Acqua Cotta, 34
Beef Broth, 30
Chicken Broth, 32
Fish Soup, 37
Minestrone alla Genovese, 32
Onion Soup, 34
Pasta in Broth, 32

Stracciatella Armando, 32
Tuscan Bean Soup, 36
Tuscan Pepper and Tomato
 Soup, 34
Vegetable Soup Genoa
 Style, 32
Venetian Bean and Noodle
 Soup, 37

NOODLES
Agnollotti, 48
Bolognese Macaroni with
 Sausage, 57
Bucatini, 59
Cappelleti, 44
Dumplings, see Gnocchi
Gnocchi di Gloria, 46
Gnocchi di Poveri, 47
Gnocchi Verdi with Garlic
 Sauce, 45
Grandma's Egg Noodles, 56
Grandma's Noodle Dough, 39
Lasagne di Diana, 56
Lasagne di Signora Domasi, 54
Macaroni with Sausage,
 Bolognese, 57
Noodle Dough, 39, 56

Noodles Stuffed with Pota-
 toes, 48
Pasta in Broth, 32
Poor Man's Dumplings, 47
Potato Dumplings, see Gnocchi
Potato-Stuffed Noodles in the
 Style of Mugello, 52
Ravioli of the Bussa
 Family, 50
Spaghetti alla Carbonara
 (with Bacon), 62
Spaghetti alla Carbonera
 (Shellfish Sauce), 60
Spaghetti Scogliera (with Sea-
 food), 59
Spaghetti with Olive Sauce, 60
Spaghetti with Tuna, 59
Stuffed Noodles, 47-53
Tagliatelle, 41
Tagliatelle di Uova alla
 Nonna, 56
Tortelli alla Mugellana, 52
Tortellini, 47
Tortelloni Romagnoli, 53
Vermicelli with Mussels or
 Clams, 62

SAUCES

Besciamella, 54
Bolognese Meat Sauce, 40
Carbonera Sauce, 60
Garlic Sauce, 45
Green Sauce for Boiled Meat, 94
Meat Sauce, 40
Meat Sauce for Lasagne, 54
Mornay Sauce, 76
Mornay Sauce, Modified, 80
Pesto alla Genovese, 42
Pesto Sauce for Minestrone, 34
Ragù, 40, 54
Ragù di Granchio, 91
Salsa Picante, 122
Spaghetti Sauce with Giblets, 42
Tomato Sauce, 62
White Sauce, 54

RICE AND CORNMEAL

Black Rice, 65
Cornmeal, Cooked, 68
  see also Polenta
Cornmeal Pie, 70
Polenta, 68
Polenta and the Birds That Got
  Away, 70
Polenta Pasticciata, 70
Polenta with Small Birds, 69
Rice, Black, 65
Rice Salad, 17
Rice with Chard Tuscan Style, 66
Rice with Mushrooms, 66
Rice with Mushrooms and
  Sausage, 66
Rice with Peas, 63
Rice with Seafood, 65
Riso, see Rice
Riso Carbonera, 65

Risotto, 63
Risotto alla Milanese, 65

EGGS

Crespelle, see Pancakes
Eggs Florentine Style, 72
Eggs Parma Style, 74
Eggs Turin Style, 71
Frittata with Clams or
  Mussels, 74
Frittata with Mushrooms and
  Peas, 74
Omelettes, see Frittatas
Pancakes, Rolled Milan-Style, 76

FISH

Anchovies, Marinated Fresh, 21
Baked Mussels with Bread
  Crumbs, 91
Calamari, see Squid
Clams, Frittata, 74
Clams with Vermicelli, 62
Cod Livorno Style, 84
Crab in its Shell, 20
Crab Sauce, 91
Crayfish, Grilled, 86
Dried Cod Livorno Style, 84
Fish Fry, 79
Fish Stew Livorno Style, 78
Fresh Cod Livorno Style, 84
Fried Squid, 88
Frittata with Clams or
  Mussels, 74
Fritto Misto, 79
Grilled Crayfish, 86
Marinated Fresh Anchovies, 21
Mussels, Baked with Bread
  Crumbs, 91
Mussels, Frittata, 74

Mussels with Vermicelli, 62
Oysters Gratinée, 22
Prawns from the Antica Car-
  bonera, 86
Prawns Venetian Style, 22
Rice with Seafood, 65
Salmon, Stuffed, 82
Scampi alla Carbonera, 86
Scampi, see also Prawns
Sole Florentine Style, 80
Spaghetti alla Carbonera (Shell-
  fish), 60
Spaghetti from the Reefs, 59
Spaghetti with Shellfish
  Sauce, 60
Spaghetti with Tuna, 59
Squid and Celery Salad, 19
Squid, Fried, 88
Squid Stuffed with Little
  Squids, 88
Stuffed Salmon, 82
Stuffed Trout, 82
Swordfish with Anchovy, 79
Trout, Stuffed, 82
Tuna Fish Sausage, 81
Tuna, with Spaghetti, 59
Vermicelli with Mussels or
  Clams, 62

MEATS

Armando's Tripe Florentine
  Style, 109
Beef, Braised Burgamo Style, 98
Beef Pot Roast, 100
Beef, Roast, Genoa Style, 97
Beef, Stuffed Roast, 97
Beef, Stuffed Roast with Cheese
  Omelette, 98

Boiled Meat and Potatoes, Bergamo Style, 94
Boiled Meat, Green Sauce for, 94
Bolognese Meat Sauce, 60
Braised Beef, Bergamo Style, 98
Crescents Bologna Style, 26
Florentine Steaks in the Manner of Sostanza, 101
Grilled Pork Chops, 112
Lamb, Tuscan, with Greek Type Olives, 108
Liver Venetian Style, 111
Macaroni with Sausage, Bolognese, 57
Meatballs with Marsala Wine, 95
Meat Sauce, 40
Meat Sauce for Lasagne, 54
Ossobuco, 102
Pork and Beans Bergamo Style, 112
Pork Chops, Grilled, 112
Pork Chops Modena Style, 111
Rice with Mushrooms and Sausage, 66
Roast Beef Genoa Style, 97
Roasted Veal Steak, 101
Rolled Scaloppine Delight, 107
Sausage, with Macaroni, Bolognese, 57
Sausage, with Rice and Mushrooms, 66
Sausage, with Rice (Risotto alla Milanese), 65
Scaloppine, see Veal
Spaghetti alla Carbonara (Bacon), 62
Steaks, Florentine, in the Manner of Sostanza, 101

Stuffed Roast Beef, 97
Stuffed Roast Beef with Cheese Omelette, 98
Tripe Florentine Style, 109
Tripe in Green Sauce, 109
Tuscan Lamb with Greek-Type Olives, 108
Veal Cutlets Milan Style, 104
Veal in Tuna Fish Sauce, 108
Veal Scaloppine in Madeira Wine, 106
Veal Scaloppine in Marsala Wine, 104
Veal Scaloppine Livorno Style, 107
Veal Scaloppine, Rolled Delight, 107
Veal Shin Bone, 102
Veal Steak, Roasted, 101
Vitello, see Veal

POULTRY
Chicken Breasts, Sostanza, 116
Chicken Breasts, Stuffed, 114
Chicken in Beer, 120
Chicken Kabobs, 116
Chicken Livers on Toast, 24
Chicken Marengo, 116
Chicken Necks, Stuffed, 118
Chicken, Stewed, 118
Chicken with Bell Pepper, 117
Chicken with Lemon, 118
Devil's Hot Chicken, 115
Duck in Chianti Wine, 122
Duck, Spicy, Treviso Style, 122
Giblets with Spaghetti Sauce, 42
Grilled Squabs, 121
Home-Style Stuffed Chicken Necks, 118

Polenta and the Birds That Got Away, 70
Polenta with Small Birds, 69
Spaghetti Sauce with Giblets, 42
Spicy Duck Treviso Style, 122
Squabs, Grilled, 121
Stewed Chicken, 118
Stuffed Chicken Breasts, 114
Turkey with Sausage, 120

VEGETABLES
Artichokes with Potatoes, 133
Asparagus, Breaded, Pavia Style, 127
Asparagus Florentine Style, 127
Beans in a Bottle, 131
Beans in the Style of Little Birds, 132
Breaded Asparagus Pavia Style, 127
Broccoli and Cauliflower Milan Style, 128
Cabbage, Wilted, Salad, 17
Cauliflower with Anchovy Sauce, 126
Celery Milan Style, 128
Chard, with Rice Tuscan Style, 66
Eggplant in the Style of Parma, 130
Fava Beans, Raw, 15
Fennel and Tomato Salad, 15
Fennel Mold, 134
Fried Zucchini, 129
Frittata with Mushrooms and Peas, 74
Italian Squash, Stuffed, 129
Lentil Stew, 133
Mushrooms and Peas, Frittata, 74

Mushrooms, with Rice, 66
Peas, and Mushrooms,
    Frittata, 74
Peas, with Rice, 63
Potato Dumplings, See Noodles
Raw Fava Beans, 15
Rice with Chard Tuscan
    Style, 66
Rice with Mushrooms, 66
Rice with Peas, 63
Spinach with Anchovies, 126
Spinach with Lemon, 125
Stuffed Italian Squash, 129
Tomato and Fennel Salad, 15
Tomato Sauce, 62
Wilted Cabbage Salad, 17
Zucchini, Fried, 129

DESSERTS AND PASTRIES
Baked Custard, 144
Brandy and Custard Cake, 141
Brutti Ma Buoni, 158
Carnival Fritters, 163
Cats' Tongues, 162

Cheese and Brandy Icebox
    Cake, 138
Cheese Pie, 149
Chocolate Cream, 160
Chocolate Souffle', 144
Coffee and Cream Dessert, 143
Coffee Mousse, 144
Cookies with Preserves, 160
Cornets, 158
Creme Caramel, 144
Drunken Flat Cake, 147
Èclairs with Pastry Custard, 152
Flaky Crooked Pastries, 157
Flaky Pastries with Custard, 157
Florentine Carnival Cake, 146
Friars in Butter, 162
Fruit Tarts Milan Style, 151
Horns of Plenty, 158
Ice Cream Cake, 140
Italian Dunking Cookies, 159
Lady's Kisses, 160
Marzipan Cake, 150
Marzipan Cookies, 160
Melon with Marsala Wine, 137
Mixed Fruit Delight, 138
Nuts and Citron Cake, 149
Pasta Brisée, 72

Pastry Custard, 141, 152
Peaches and Cream Cake, 145
Pie Crust, 72
Piedmontese Cake with Choco-
    late Frosting, 145
Piedmontese Deep Fried
    Cookies, 162
Piedmontese Pudding, 143
Pineapple Cake, 150
Pound Cake, 140
Puff Pastry, 154
Quick Puff Pastry, 154
Rice and Milk Fritters, 163
Ricotta Cheese and Brandy
    Cake, 140
Short Pastry, 150
Sponge Cake, 141
Strawberries and Cream, 136
Thousand Layer Cake, 157
Ugly But Good Cookies, 158
Wine Custard, 138
Zabaglione, 138
Zuccotto, 138-140
Zuppa Inglese, 141

ABOUT THE AUTHOR

Violeta Autumn has led a diverse life. She spent her childhood in Peru, graduated with a degree in architecture from the University of Oklahoma in 1953, and now lives with her husband and son in Sausalito, California. Consistent with her varied background is her versatility. Mrs. Autumn is a licensed and practicing architect. She is a painter, having executed several murals, illustrated textbooks and exhibited her paintings in numerous one-man shows in the United States and abroad. To cap these talents, she is an excellent cook. The recipes and sketches in this book are the result of her extensive travels through Northern Italy. She is also the author of *A Russian Jew Cooks in Peru*, previously published by 101 Productions.